COMMUNITY LAW IN THE FRENCH COURTS

The Law of Treaties in Modern Attire

COMMUNITY LAW IN THE FRENCH COURTS

THE LAW OF TREATIES IN MODERN ATTIRE

by

ERIC E. BERGSTEN

SPRINGER-SCIENCE+BUSINESS MEDIA, B.V. / 1973

Originally published by Martinus Nijhoff, The Hague, Netherlands in 1973

ISBN 978-94-015-0034-0 ISBN 978-94-015-0503-1 (eBook)
DOI 10.1007/978-94-015-0503-1

ACKNOWLEDGEMENTS

This manuscript was originally prepared as a dissertation for the degree of Doctor of Comparative Law at the University of Chicago. I want to thank the members of my committee, Professors Gerhard Casper, Chairman, Max Rheinstein and Kenneth Culp Davis, for their comments and help in preparing the final version of the dissertation.

I owe a special debt of gratitude to Professor Rheinstein who introduced me to the study of French law as a student in the Foreign Law Program. The years have shown how much we who have been in the Program learned under his tutelage. Even more important, however, is the compassion and understanding he has always shown towards "his" students, among whom I am very proud to be counted.

Among the many people to whom I owe debts of gratitude for help or for forbearance throughout the seemingly endless preparation of this manuscript are my wife, Jane, my three children, Steven, Kristin and Britt, my secretary, Mrs. Ruth Bonar, and the acquisitions librarian in the Law Library of the University of Iowa, Mrs. Katherine Belgum.

Eric E. Bergsten

ABBREVIATIONS FOR COMMONLY CITED OR NON-ENGLISH LANGUAGE PUBLICATIONS

Act. Jur. Dr. Ad.	Actualité Juridique: Droit Administratif
Ann. Fr. Dr. Int'l	Annuaire Français de Droit International
Bull. Civ.	Bulletin des Décisions de la Cour de Cassation, Chambre Civile
CCH Comm. Mkt. Rep.	Commerce Clearing House, Common Market Reporter
Clunet	Journal du Droit International
Comm. Mkt. L. R.	Common Market Law Reports
Comm. Mkt. L. Rev.	Common Market Law Review
D. (Has also appeared as D.A., D.C., D.H., D.P. and D.S.)	Recueil Dalloz de Doctrine, de Jurisprudence et de Législation
D. Rép.	Dalloz, Jurisprudence Générale, Répertoire de Législation, de Doctrine et de Jurisprudence
E.E.C. J.O.	European Economic Community, Journal Officiel
Eur. Parl. Docs.	European Parliament, Documents
Gaz. Pal.	Gazette du Palais
J.C.P.	Juris Classeur Périodique, La Semaine Juridique
J.O.	Journal Officiel de la Républic Française
Jour. Pal.	Journal du Palais
Rec. Cons. d'Ét.	Recueil des Décisions du Conseil d'État
Rec. de la Cour	Recueil de la Jurisprudence de la Cour de Justice des Communautés Européennes
Recueil des Cours	Académie de Droit International, Recueil des Cours
Rev Cr. D.I.P.	Revue Critique de Droit International Privé
Rev. Dr. Int'l Pr.	Revue de Droit International Privé
Rev. Dr. Pub.	Revue de Droit Public et de la Science Politique en France et à l'Etranger
Rev. Gen. Dr. Int'l Pub.	Revue Générale de Droit International Public
Rev. Tr. Dr. Eur.	Revue Trimestrielle de Droit Européen
S.	Recueil Sirey

TABLE OF CONTENTS

INTRODUCTION

The European Communities are only two decades old. The most important of the three Communities, the European Economic Community (EEC), is even younger, having come into existence in 1958.[1] Two decades have been hardly enough time to have more than reached, much less settled, the important questions of the relationship between Community law and institutions and those of the Member States.

Among the most challenging of the questions is the extent to which the courts of the Member States will fulfill the obligation of safeguarding the rights created by the Treaty of Rome in favor of private persons, both individual and corporate, an obligation which the Court of Justice of the European Communities has said rests upon the national courts. This obligation flows naturally, though not necessarily, from the commitment of the Court of Justice to an effective Community. However, the result depends on that commitment, and there is a natural concern that the national courts may not share the commitment to an effective Community to a degree necessary to fulfill their obligations under Community law as those obligations have been defined by the Court of Justice.

In order to fulfill their obligations to Community law the courts of the Member States will have to solve some serious problems, and do it with comparatively little help from the Court of Justice. The most important of those problems at this stage of Community development is the need to reconcile the supremacy of Community law and the finality of its interpretation by the Court of Justice with traditional learning about the status of treaties in the courts. This paper discusses that problem as it arises in the French courts.

[1] Treaty of Rome instituting the European Economic Community of March 25, 1957 (Treaty of Rome), ratified in France by law No. 57-880 of Aug. 2, 1957, J.O. 1957. 7716, D. 1957. L. 241, ratified by decree No. 58-84 of Jan. 28, 1958, J.O. 1958. 118, D. 1958. L. 73. The official English language version of the Treaty is available in Sweet & Maxwell's European Community Treaties 71 (1972).

All references to the "Communities", "Community law" or to treaty articles refer to the European Economic Community or to the Treaty of Rome unless the context otherwise requires.

CHAPTER I

THE COMMUNITY OBLIGATION

It has been difficult for the courts of the Member States to adjust to their obligations under Community law. Some of the problems are technical. Domestic court procedure, which has evolved to handle legal problems as they are framed in the national legal system, is not always adequate to the demands of Community law.[1] Community law terms and concepts must be interpreted in the light of the overall purpose of the Communities, i.e., the uniting of the economies of the Member States, a problem foreign to the experience of the national legal systems. National courts have been called upon to make economic analyses for which they have not been trained.

The most serious problem, however, is political. The courts of the Member States have been told they must recognize the supremacy of Community law over their national law.[2] In addition, article 177 of the Treaty of Rome prohibits the national courts of last resort from deciding questions of interpretation of Community law but requires them to request an interpretation from the Court of Justice.[3] They are told by the partisans of the Communities that they must do this not only to assure the unity of interpretation among all the Member States, a reason which does not threaten them, but also because they are not technically competent to understand fully the significance of Community law and because they must demonstrate their allegiance to the Community legal system and to the functional supremacy of Community law over their national law, both very threatening ideas indeed.[4]

[1] Some of the procedural problems for the French Conseil d'Etat are suggested by Mme Questiaux in her conclusions as *commissaire du gouvernment* in Petitjean, Conseil d'Etat, Feb. 10, 1967, 3 Rev. Tr. Dr. Eur. 681, 690 (1967).

[2] Costa v. E.N.E.L., Cour de Justice des Communautés Européennes, July 15, 1964, 10 Rec. de la Cour 1141, [1961-1966 Transfer Binder] CCH Comm. Mkt. Rep. ¶ 8023.

[3] Where any such question [of interpretation] is raised in a case pending before a court or tribunal of a Member State, against whose decisions there is no judicial remedy under national law, that court or tribunal shall bring the matter before the Court of Justice.

[4] Although the statement in the text puts the proposition more sharply than is to be found in the literature, see Delvolvé, *Le Pouvoir judiciaire et le Traité de Rome ou la diplomatie des juges*, J.C.P. 1968. I. 2184; Gaudet, *Exposé devant la Commission juridique en sa réunion du 18 février 1965*, 1 Rev. Tr. Dr. Eur. 198 (1965); Pépy, *L'article 177 du Traité de Rome et les juridictions françaises*, 52 Rev. Cr. D.I.P. 475, 488 et seq. (1963).

Nevertheless, they remain national courts with all that that implies. Questions of allegiance do indeed arise, and it is not a foregone conclusion that the national courts should be loyal to the Communities as a political system absent a clear statement to that effect by the political institutions of the state. It is fair to say that the national political institutions, and particularly those of France, have been ambivalent towards the political destination of the Communities. This has not eased the task of the national courts to reconcile the conflicting demands of Community law and national law.

The natural tendency of the national courts has been to see Community law as a specialized branch of international law. The fundamental texts of the Communities after all are treaties, treaties which were negotiated, signed, ratified and published in the same manner as other treaties.

The national courts are comfortable with treaties. They have doctrines which explain the manner in which self-executing treaties create domestic law, the manner in which they are to be interpreted and their relationship to other domestic law. If Community law were no more than a special form of the law of treaties, it would cause fewer problems for the national courts.

There are, however, significant differences between Community law and ordinary treaties which make it difficult to transpose the traditional law of treaties to the consideration of Community law. One major difference lies in the manner in which ordinary treaties and Community law create postive domestic law. The domestic law effect of an ordinary treaty is restricted to the terms of the treaty itself and can arise only to the extent that a provision is self-executing or the state enacts legislation to fulfill its treaty obligations.

In contrast, the Community legal system resembles a federal system. The Treaties, as does our Constitution, contain some self-executing substantive law, but their primary function is to provide an institutional structure for the future operation of the Communities. Most Community law is a derived secondary law enacted either by the Council of Ministers or by the Commission. Although Community law in the form of a directive requires the Member State to take some action before it becomes effective law within the domestic legal system,[5] Council and Commission regulations "have general

[5] In spite of the Treaty provision in art. 189, a directive can be directly applicable within a Member State if it creates an objective rule of law which is susceptible of application without the intervention of the Member State. S.A.C.E. S.p.a. v. Ministère des finances de la République italienne, Cour de Justice des Communautés Européennes, Dec. 17, 1970, 16 Rec. de la Cour 1213, 2 CCH Comm. Mkt. Rep. ¶ 8117.

application [and are] binding in [their] entirety and directly applicable in all Member States."[6] While called regulations, they serve the same function as do statutes in the domestic legal systems.

A second major difference between Community law and ordinary treaties relates to the context in which individual provisions must be interpreted. Ordinary treaties are generally isolated acts unrelated to one another. Certainly, they borrow language from other treaties between the same or different states. In some cases a network of treaties, exchanges of diplomatic notes and other forms of international agreement are developed on a given subject. But neither the standardization of certain treaty provisions nor the occasional network of agreements is sufficient to create an integrated law. As a result the national courts legitimately tend to interpret treaties as modifications of and in the light of their domestic law and not as a separate coherent substantive law.[7]

Community law does not have the same fragmentary nature. The myriad regulations, directives, decisions, recommendations and opinions implementing the Treaties have created a body of law which has a life of its own. Single provisions often cannot be understood by themselves, nor by reference only to the text of which they are a part. They require interpretation as part of the total corpus of Community law.

A third difference arises out of the first two. The Communities have a dynamic political purpose which goes far beyond the agreements which were originally reached in the Treaties themselves. In form the Member States have agreed to agree on a whole range of subjects. Although there is no agreement on the ultimate political form into which the Communities should evolve, there is agreement that the ultimate goal is "to lay the foundations of an ever closer union among the peoples of Europe"[8] and that the first step is to establish a Common Market.[9] The history of the fifteen years since the EEC came into existence have been years of progress towards that goal. The existence of such a goal requires a commensurate teleological interpretation of the existing Community law.

A fourth distinction is that most Community law has existed in four official

[6] Art. 189. In 1971 the Communities adopted 2862 regulations.

[7] 1 Bartin, Principes de droit international privé ¶ 53 (1930); 1 Niboyet, Traité de droit international privé français ¶ 21 (2e éd. 1947).

[8] Preamble, Treaty of Rome.

[9] Art. 2.

languages and after January 1, 1973, will exist in six official languages.[10] To a degree this is an old problem. Bilateral treaties are usually equally valid in the official languages of the two contracting parties. Treaties sponsored by the United Nations are promulgated in the five official U.N. languages and many other multilateral treaties in Western political society are official in both French and English. Therefore, it is rare to find a treaty in only one official language unless that is the language of all the contracting parties.

The difference between Community law and the general law of treaties lies in the attitude of the national courts to the texts in the other languages. Although international courts have long faced the problems associated with divergent texts in the different languages and scholars have consistently pointed out discrepancies in the terms used in different versions of the same treaty,[11] few national courts seem to be aware of the text of treaties in any language but their own, and, indeed, may be precluded by their national law from relying upon them.[12]

This result is not acceptable for Community law. The volume of Community law assures the existence of numerous discrepancies, not only because of errors in translation but because legal terms are words of art which often have no exact counterpart in other languages. Each discrepancy represents a lack of uniformity where uniformity has been sought. The lack of uniformity means preferential or discriminatory treatment for some Community nationals. Therefore, the courts of the Member States must hold themselves responsible for the meaning of the provision in question in all the official

[10] The Treaty establishing the European Coal and Steel Community is official only in the French language. The Treaty for the Accession of Denmark, Ireland, Norway and the United Kingdom is official not only in the original four languages, but also in Danish, Irish, Norwegian and English. As part of the accession process the Treaties creating the European Economic Community and the European Atomic Energy Community were drawn up in Danish, Irish, Norwegian and English and are "authentic under the same conditions as the original texts of the Treaties referred to above." Art. 160, Act concerning the Conditions of Accession and the Adjustments to the Treaties. Community secondary law of general application adopted after January 1, 1973 is official in six languages, Danish, Dutch, English, French, German and Italian. For a discussion of the problems concerning the interpretation of plurilingual treaties in relation to the treaties establishing the European Communities, see Stevens, *The Principle of Linguistic Equality in Judicial Proceedings and in the Interpretation of Plurilingual Legal Instruments: The Regime Linguistique in the Court of Justice of the European Communities*, 62 NW. U. L. Rev. 701 (1967); Dickschat, *Problèmes d'interprétation des traités européens résultant de leur plurilinguisme*, 4 Revue Belge de Droit International 40 (1968).

[11] E.g., Germer, *Interpretation of Plurilingual Treaties: A Study of Article 33 of the Vienna Convention on the Law of Treaties*, 11 Harv. Int. L. J. 400 (1970), and authorities cited therein.

[12] Malaurie, *Le droit français et la diversité des langues*, 92 Clunet 565, 589 (1965); Hardy, *The Interpretation of Plurilingual Treaties by International Courts and Tribunals*, 37 British Year Book of International Law 72, 137 (1961). However, some national courts have relied on a text in a foreign language rather than the language of the forum. *Ibid.*; United States v. Percheman, 32 U.S. (7 Pet.) 41 (1833).

languages. If there are any doubts as to the meaning of a provision in any one of them, the national courts should use the procedure available under article 177 for a prejudicial interpretation. Perhaps this would not have been seen as such an important issue if it were not that there are subtle but significant differences in the meaning of several key provisions in the Treaty itself, provisions which obviously are not subject to correction by a *rectificatif* in an early issue of the Official Journal of the European Communities.[13]

A fifth distinction between Community law and the general law of treaties noted by some is that there is an established judicial procedure under articles 169-171 for the determination whether a "Member State has failed to fulfil an obligation under this Treaty," a procedure which goes beyond those generally available for the alleged violation of ordinary treaties. It can be expected, and has indeed been the case, that most actions under articles 169-171 allege the existence of national law in violation of a provision of Community law.[14] Therefore, the existence of such a procedure can be seen as evidence that Community law is superior to conflicting national law.

This argument can easily be refuted. It is standard doctrine that a national statute cannot abrogate the international obligation of a treaty. Whatever may be the domestic consequences of the statute, an international tribunal will consider a statute in conflict with a treaty merely as the means by which the treaty was breached. Similarly, a judgment by the Court of Justice that a national statute is in conflict with Community law is declaratory only and does not of itself invalidate, repeal or annul it. That action must be taken by an appropriate institution of the Member State. Absent the authority to annul the offending national statute, there is no intrinsic reason why articles 169-171 must be seen to provide more than the traditional authority of an international tribunal to announce that a State has failed in its obligations under international law.

Nevertheless, even if the existence of articles 169-171 does not necessarily lead to the conclusion that Community law is formally superior to national law, the procedure is intended to bring national law into conformity with Community law, and it has had that effect. In late 1970 the Commission

[13] The most obvious example is found in article 85. See, e.g., Ellis, *L'interprétation du mot "affecter" dans l'art. 85 § 1er du traité de la Communauté économique européenne par rapport aux mots "empêcher" "restreindre" ou "fausser le jeu de la concurence,"* D. 1963. chron. 221.

[14] EEC Commission v. Italy, Cour de Justice des Communautés Européennes, Feb. 17, 1970, 16 Rec. de la Cour 25, [1967-1970 Transfer Binder] CCH Comm. Mkt. Rep. ¶ 8097, was the first case in which the action was brought under article 169 for a failure other than the existence of domestic law in conflict with Community law. See the conclusions of Advocate General Gand, 16 Rec. de la Cour at 42, [1967-1970 Transfer Binder] CCH Com. Mkt. Rep. at 8391. The case involved the failure of Italy to pay refunds to exporters of certain agricultural products as required by Community regulations.

reported that in only one case had the Member State failed to execute the adverse judgement of the Court of Justice within a reasonable period of time, even when the judgment required the repeal of a statute.[15] In that case, which involved a tax on the exportation of artistic property to the other Member States, the Italian Government submitted the necessary draft legislation to the Parliament in sufficient time but a continuing parliamentary crisis delayed its passage. The Commission's only legal recourse was to begin a new procedure under articles 169-171, this time for Italy's failure to execute the prior judgment. Prior to judgment in the second case Italy adopted a decree-law repealing the offending tax retroactive to January 1, 1962 and provided for the reimbursement of the taxes collected after that date.[16] A week later the Court of Justice rendered its decision in which it simply noted that Italy was no longer in violation of its obligation to execute a decision of the Court of Justice pursuant to article 171.[17]

While the inability of the Communities to execute the judgments of the Court of Justice against the Member States is a weakness which may have serious consequences in the future, to date the record indicates that the Member States have been willing to honor the obligation to execute a judgment of the Court of Justice rendered under the procedure of articles 169-171. Therefore, the practical result is that the functional supremacy of Community law over national law has been established through the procedure of articles 169-171, whatever may be the formal hierarchy between the two.[18]

While articles 169-171 have served to assure the functional supremacy of Community law on those occasions when they have been invoked, by their very nature they are apt to reach only a limited number of the violations of Community law by the Member States. The most obvious limitation has been the unwillingness of the Member States to file actions against one another under article 170. States are not used to settling their disputes with one another through litigation. Litigation implies that the moving party is not only insisting on close adherence to the letter of the law or of the agreement today but is willing to abide by it in the future. Rather than placing themselves in

[15] Response to Parliamentary Question 238/70, 13 E.E.C. J.O. C 138/12 (1970).

[16] Response to Parliamentary Question 326/72, 15 E.E C. J.O. 120/12 (1972).

[17] EEC Commission v. Italy, Cour de Justice des Communautés Européennes, July 13, 1972, 18 Rec. de la Cour —, 15 E.E.C. J.O. C 115/16 (1972).

[18] Although the same is probably true of most judgments of international tribunals, there are two striking differences. Most international tribunals receive their jurisdiction in an individual case from the voluntary submission of the dispute to litigation. However, articles 169-171 give the Court of Justice a mandatory jurisdiction until such time as a Member State has withdrawn from the Communities. Secondly, article 169 authorizes a Community institution, the Commission, to commence the proceedings.

such a restricted position, states generally prefer to negotiate their differences and to change the rules of the game if one party absolutely insists.

The Commission has been considerably more active in using its authority under article 169. By late 1972 it had commenced 29 actions in the Court of Justice.[19] Even this record is far from what is necessary to assure the compliance with Community law by the Member States. Nor is the record apt to improve greatly.

One of the reasons lies in the political status of the Commission vis-à-vis the Member States and the Council of Ministers. Although the members of the Commission have often been men with considerable political experience in their own countries, as Commissioners they have no independent political constituency. The Communities have been fortunate that the men appointed to the Commission have performed their duties with the independence called for by the Treaty.[20] However, they are appointed by the Member States for only four year terms[21] and reappointment has been denied several Commissioners who became too independent. The defeats suffered by the High Authority in the coal crisis of 1958-59 and by the Commission during the crisis over agricultural financing in 1965-66 have made the Commission reluctant to engage a Member State in a contest, even before the Court of Justice, on a matter which the Member State deems of vital interest to it.

Furthermore, the Commission's staff is limited in its manpower and cannot attempt to document every intentional and unintentional violation of Community law. It must perforce choose from among the many apparent violations which come to its attention, those violations which are important, are not too politically sensitive, and which it can expect to substantiate. By late 1972 the Commission had lost only three cases under article 169.[22] While this is a commendable record in respect to its ability to choose its cases, document them and argue them to the Court, it also suggests that the Commission has ignored other violations in which success was less certain.[23]

[19] By the end of 1969 the procedure envisaged by article 169 had been invoked by the Commission 214 times, leading to 72 "reasoned opinions," and 23 actions before the Court of Justice resulting in 14 decisions. Response to Parliamentary Question 501/69, 13 E.E.C. J.O. C 73/1 (1970). No information was given as to how many of the procedures begun or "reasoned opinions" related to cases still open. An additional 6 actions had been commenced in the Court of Justice by late 1972, including one case under the Euratom Treaty.

[20] Art. 10, Treaty Establishing a Single Council and a Single Commission of the European Communities, April 8, 1965, 10 E.E.C. J.O. 152/2 (1967).

[21] Art. 11, *ibid.*

[22] Response to Parliamentary Question 501/69, 13 E.E.C. J.O. C 73/1 (1970); EEC Commission v. France, Cour de Justice des Communautés Européennes, July 9, 1970, 16 Rec. de la Cour 565, 2 CCH Comm. Mkt. Rep. ¶ 8103.

[23] It was reported in January 1972 that the Commission intended to keep a closer watch on the implementing of directives by the Member States. The Commission was reported to have "about 136 cases of infringements [which] have been more or less proved or suspected by the Commission." Agence Europe, Jan. 5, 1972, No. 955 (new series), p. 4.

Individuals can neither set in motion the procedure of articles 169-171 nor force the Commission to do so.[24] This limitation is understandable. It is common in domestic legal systems to limit the standing of individuals to make direct attacks on legislation or regulations even if the legality of the legislation or regulation can be raised collaterally. It is particularly understandable that the Member States would wish to avoid having individuals make direct attacks in the Court of Justice on the conformity of domestic legislation to Community law. If an individual could sue a Member State in the Court of Justice, it would imply a greater loss of sovereignty than that which is implied by the commencement of legal action by the Commission or by another Member State.

The same basic rule is found in American constitutional law. The Eleventh Amendment to the Constitution provides that

> The Judicial power of the United States shall not be construed to extend to any suit in law or equity, commenced or prosecuted against one of the United States by Citizens of another State, or by Citizens or Subjects of any Foreign State.

The Amendment was the result of the angry reaction to the Supreme Court's decision in *Chisholm* v. *Georgia*[25] in 1793 that the federal courts had jurisdiction over a suit by a citizen of one state against another state. Over the years it has been subjected to considerable interpretation, especially in respect to the right of a citizen to bring an action in federal court against his own state and to the right of a federal court to enjoin state officials from acting under an unconstitutional statute. However, its basic thrust remains valid today; actions against the state are generally to be prosecuted in the courts of the state with the possibility of eventual review by the Supreme Court of the United States on federal grounds through the issuance of a writ of certiorari or by appeal.

Nevertheless, even if the rule is reasonable, to deny individuals standing in the Court of Justice to contest actions of a Member State alleged to be in violation of Community law leaves a definite weakness in the system. Much of Community law is directly applicable and intended to create legal rights in individuals. Because Community law deals with the regulation of the economy, a matter which has been the subject of extensive regulation by the Member States since at least the 1940s, many of the claims of interference with the rights of individuals have been directed at the actions or non-actions

[24] See Firma Alfons Lütticke GmbH v. EEC Commission, Cour de Justice des Communautés Européennes, March 1, 1966, 12 Rec. de la Cour 27, [1961-1966 Transfer Binder] CCH Comm. Mkt. Rep. ¶ 8044.

[25] 2 U.S. (2 Dall.) 419.

of a Member State. The refusal to give individuals standing in the Court of Justice to contest the denial of their rights under Community law by a Member State has reduced to that extent the value of those rights and has placed additional emphasis on the alternative remedies available to protect them.

These institutional weaknesses of articles 169-171 do not render them useless, only insufficient. They are insufficient because the very concept of Community implies adherence to jointly determined rules as expressed by the Treaties and secondary texts, and the procedure of articles 169-171 cannot guarantee such adherence.

Nor can the parliaments of the Member States be counted upon as guardians of Community law. Except for the handful of members who also sit in the European Parliament, the members of the national parliaments have little contact with or responsibility for either Community law itself, which is enacted in Brussels by the Council and the Commission, or for the national law which must be changed to fulfill the Member State's obligations under Community law. In France Parliament has delegated to the Government the authority to enact ordonnances necessary to fulfill France's obligations to the Communities.[26] This delegation grants the Government authority to legislate even in respect to matters normally reserved to the Parliament. While this practice has had the salutary effect of reducing political obstacles to the fulfillment of France's obligations under the Treaty, it has also reduced the already too limited contact between the French political process and Community development.

As the volume of Community law increases, inadvertent conflicts are more likely. Community texts are often technical, complicated, and sometimes obscure. They have been written in four languages and are now written in six. There are many possibilities for genuine disagreement over their meaning and for honest error in the drafting of national implementing laws and regulations. If the national authorities are diligent, these errors will be few and many will be found prior to enactment or before harm is done. Community officials and private individuals who are affected can also be expected to point out errors which come to their attention. But there are bound to be many instances in which differences of interpretation remain or in which harm was done before the error was corrected.

Even prompt action takes time, particularly if the offending text is legislative. Furthermore, in some percentage of the cases the legislature or the executive, as the case may be, will refuse or stall the necessary action. If the offending national text is considered binding and valid until repealed or

[26] The most recent delegation of authority is contained in law 69-1169 of Dec. 26, 1969, J.O. 1969. 12670, J.C.P. 1970. III. 36218.

modified by the legislative or executive authorities, there is no way by which individuals can secure their rights under Community law until the remedial action is taken.

Good faith adherence to the Communities by the Member States requires not only the attempt to draft appropriate legislation in the first place and the correction of errors which have crept into such legislation, but also the existence of adequate procedures by which differences in interpretation can be resolved and the errors which have already caused harm can be indemnified.

Only three broad alternatives are possible. One requires the expansion of the competence of the Court of Justice under articles 169-171. Individuals could be given standing to bring actions on the same grounds as the Commission and the Member States. The remedies available in the Court of Justice could also be broadened to authorize the annulment of national legislation in conflict with Community law and the awarding of appropriate damages. Neither amendment to articles 169-171 is conceivable absent a radical change in the present conception of the Communities.

A second alternative would amend article 177 so that the Court of Justice had the authority of a Community Supreme Court or Community Cour de Cassation to which petitions from adverse judgments of national courts could be taken as of right or at the discretion of the Court of Justice for alleged violations of Community law. Less drastic versions of this alternative would increase the likelihood that a national court would refer a prejudicial question to the Court of Justice.[27]

The third alternative, and the one which the Court of Justice on a number of occasions has said is presently required by the Treaty, is that the courts of the Member States will safeguard the rights of individuals which arise under Community law.[28] If they are to do so, four elements must be present.

First, Community law must be recognized as positive law within the legal system of the Member States. This has been no problem. All six original Member States have recognized self-executing treaties in their domestic law and the doctrine has been applied automatically to the Community Treaties. Similarly, all six have given full recognition to the rule in article 189 that regulations are directly applicable in the Member States. Although the United Kingdom has difficult theoretical problems in arriving at the same solution, it is believed that there will be few problems in practice.[29]

[27] These less drastic proposals are discussed in Chapter V.

[28] Costa v. ENEL, Cour de Justice des Communautés Européennes, July 15, 1964, 10 Rec de la Cour 1141, [1961-1966 Transfer Binder] CCH Comm. Mkt. Rep. ¶ 8023.

[29] Mitchell, Kuipers & Gall, *Constitutional Aspects of the Treaty and legislation Relating to British Membership*, 9 Comm. Mkt. L. Rev. 134 (1972).

Second, the domestic procedure must be technically adequate to adjudicate rights under Community law. This has been only a minor problem so far, but as the volume of Community law grows it will be of increasing importance.

Third, there must be adequate procedures for the interpretation of Community law so that the obligations of the Member States are clear and uniform. The mechanism devised for this purpose is found in article 177. It provides that any national court may request an interpretation of a Community text by the Court of Justice if it considers that a decision on this point is necessary in order to deliver its judgment. However, any "court or tribunal of a Member State, against whose decisions there is no judicial remedy under national law" is required to make the request. The difference in obligations arises from the desire not to overburden the Court of Justice with requests for interpretation in insignificant cases. Therefore, the obligation to request an interpretation was limited to those courts whose decisions create a case law effective throughout the state.

Fourth, the courts of the Member States must apply Community law even though it is in conflict with some provision of national law. Such conflicts are relatively rare. As noted above, the Member States have worked diligently at implementing Community law. Nevertheless, such conflicts do arise and if the courts of the Member States are to safeguard the rights of individuals under Community law, they must do so in the face of conflicting national law as well as when the task is easier.

Neither the existence of article 177 nor its use by a national court constitutes in itself an admission of the supremacy of Community law any more than do articles 169-171. If the text is involved in litigation in a national court, it must perforce be interpreted by somebody, be it the Court of Justice, the Ministry of Foreign Affairs, as is the general practice for other treaties in France, or the national court in which the litigation is taking place. In theory, at least, conflicts in priority between the treaty and the domestic statutory law need be resolved only after the two texts have been interpreted in such a way that there is indeed a conflict.

In practice the result is otherwise. A court which must choose between two different 'laws,' whether they emanate from the same or from different sources, will normally attempt to reconcile any apparent conflicts. Therefore, if one of the "laws" is clear in its terms or has been made clear by a prior interpretation, and if the second text can be interpreted in good faith in a manner which will avoid the conflict, the court will usually adopt this interpretation. It may do this even though the second text is pre-eminent in the hierarchy of norms, unless the court is the special guardian of the preeminent text. Therefore, the determination of which text will be interpreted first, and by whom if that is in issue, will often determine which of the two norms will be applied.[30] As a practical matter it would be very difficult for a national court to refuse to apply a Community text as interpreted by the Court of Justice if the national court had requested the interpretation. It would be difficult even though that text was in conflict with a national statute enacted subsequent to the enactment of the Community text.

This became apparent as early as the second case which the Court of Justice considered under article 177.[31] In 1959 the Netherlands adopted a statute by which it ratified the Brussels Protocol to the Benelux Convention. The Protocol modified the tariff nomenclature in use by the Benelux countries. As an incidental result of the modifications in nomenclature there was an increase in the tariff on certain products above that in effect on January 1, 1958, while at the same time there was a decrease in the tariff on other products. An importing firm by the name of Van Gend & Loos protested the imposition of the increased duties on goods coming from Germany and, when the protest was disallowed by the customs inspector, appealed to the Tariefcommissie, the administrative court of last resort in fiscal matters.

The Tariefcommissie asked two questions of the Court of Justice: (1) "Does article 12, which requires the Member States to abstain from introducing between themselves any new customs duties or from increasing those in effect on January 1, 1958, give direct rights to individuals enforceable in the courts rather than merely create an obligation between the Member States?" (2) "If the answer is in the affirmative, is the modification of the tariff structure in this case an increase of the type prohibited by article 12?"

The Netherlands Government, which submitted comments pursuant to article 20 of the Protocol on the Statute of the Court of Justice,[32] resisted the consideration of the questions by the Court of Justice on the grounds that an alleged violation of the Treaty by a Member State could be submitted to the Court of Justice for censure only by the procedure specified in articles 169 and 170 on the initiative of the Commission or of a Member State. The Court of Justice could not be called upon to make such a determination under the procedure for a prejudicial interpretation of the Treaty under article 177.

[30] This point is vividly illustrated by the history of the confrontation between the French courts and the Ministry of Foreign Affairs in respect to the lease legislation and the *carte de commerçant* which is described in Chapter III.

[31] N.V. Algemene Transport- en Expeditie Onderneming van Gend & Loos v. The Netherlands Fiscal Administration, Cour de Justice des Communautés Européennes, Feb. 5, 1963, 9 Rec. de la Cour 1, [1961-1966 Transfer Binder] CCH Comm. Mkt. Rep. ¶ 8008.

[32] In the cases governed by article 177 of this Treaty, ...the parties, the Member States, the Commission and, where appropriate, the Council, shall be entitled to submit statements of case or written observations to the Court.

The Belgian Government took a somewhat different approach. It argued that the only question really to be answered was which of two statutes the Tariefcommissie must apply, the statute of December 16, 1959, which ratified the Brussels Protocol, or the statute of December 5, 1957, which ratified the Treaty establishing the EEC. It argued that this was a typical question of domestic law within the sole jurisdiction of the courts of the Netherlands.

The Court of Justice rejected both arguments. It drew a sharp distinction between interpretation of the Treaty, for which it said it is competent, and any decision either that the Netherlands was in violation of the treaty, which it could render only under the procedure of articles 169 or 170, or in respect to the application of the Treaty according to the principles of internal Netherlands law, for which the courts of the Netherlands alone are competent.

Having decided that it could answer the questions, it then went on to hold that article 12 was directly applicable and "enures to the benefit of citizens whose individual rights the courts should protect." Secondly, it held that a prohibited increase in the effective tariff levied on a product imported from another Member State "can arise from a tariff reorganization resulting in the product's being classified under a more heavily taxed position as well as from an increase in the customs rate applied." In accordance with the position it had taken that its sole authority under article 177 was to interpret Community law and not to apply it, the Court of Justice left it up to the Tariefcommissie to determine whether the application of higher duties as a result of the tariff reclassification in this case was in fact a violation of article 12.

It was obvious what result the Court of Justice desired when the Tariefcommissie reconsidered the case, and it had every reason to believe that this result would be achieved.[33] Although the potential conflict between the Treaty of Rome and the Brussels Protocol was evident, no one had any vital interest in pursuing the matter. The Treaty of Rome was in many respects an outgrowth of the Benelux Convention and any conflicts between the two were technical in nature rather than the expression of fundamental differences in public policy. The amount of tax revenue involved was minimal. The increased duties which had resulted from the change in nomenclature were incidental to the major purpose of unifying and rationalizing the complex tariff schedules. Moreover, the decision of the Court of Justice related only to imports from the other Member States. These duties had already been reduced and were due to disappear completely by the end of the transitional period. In the meantime the decision was a precedent which was equally valid for all the Benelux partners.

[33] According to the records at the Court of Justice the action was settled without further judicial proceedings in accordance with the Court's opinion.

Van Gend & Loos illustrated how useful the procedure of article 177 could be in establishing the effective supremacy of Community law. *Costa* v. *E.N.E.L.* illustrated just how weak that procedure might be if the national courts were not willing to recognize Community law as something different from ordinary treaty law.[34]

By a law of December 6, 1962, Italy nationalized the production and distribution of electric energy. Costa, a shareholder in one of the companies which had had some of its facilities nationalized, brought an action before a Justice of the Peace in Milan for a declaration that he was not liable for an electric bill amounting to 1,925 lire (approximately $3.08 at the time) that he had received from the new national electric utility.

He alleged that the statute nationalizing the electric industry was contrary to a number of provisions of the Italian Constitution. He also alleged that it was contrary to the Treaty of Rome and that the Treaty was made superior to any ordinary law by article 11 of the Italian Constitution.[35]

In accordance with Italian procedure the Justice of the Peace referred the constitutional questions to the Italian Constitutional Court, including the question whether the statute nationalizing the electric industry violated article 11 of the Constitution. Costa in turn requested the Constitutional Court to ask the Court of Justice to interpret the articles of the Treaty which he alleged were violated by the statute.

The Constitutional Court refused to do so. It acknowledged "that the State is bound to honor its obligations." However, "the violation of a treaty even if it results in [liability of the State under international law] does not detract from the [internal] validity of [the] conflicting law."[36] Therefore, since the Italian courts are bound to apply a statute even if it conflicts with an earlier treaty, the Constitutional Court did not consider it necessary to request an interpretation of the Treaty of Rome from the Court of Justice.

Normally that should have ended the Community law aspects of the case. However, the reference of questions to the Constitutional Court did not deprive the Justice of the Peace of his jurisdiction over the case. After he had referred the questions, but prior to the decision of the Constitutional Court, the Justice of the Peace referred another set of questions to the Court of Justice asking for an interpretation of the Treaty.

[34] July 15, 1964, 10 Rec. de la Cour 1141, [1961-1966 Transfer Binder] CCH Comm. Mkt. Rep. ¶ 8023.

[35] "[Italy] agrees, on conditions of equality with other states, to such limitation of sovereignty as may be necessary for a system calculated to ensure peace and justice between Nations: it promotes and encourages international organizations having such ends in view." III Peaslee; Constitutions of Nations 501 (Rev. 3rd ed. 1968).

[36] Rac. Uff. Corte Cost. 82 (1964), 87 Foro Ital. I, 465 (1964), English translation in [1964] Comm. Mkt. L. R. 425.

The Italian Government objected to the competence of the Court of Justice on the same grounds, *inter alia*, as had the Belgian Government in *Van Gend & Loos*, namely that national constitutional law and not Community law determined which of two conflicting texts were to be applied by a national court.[37] The argument had considerably more force than in *Van Gend & Loos*. In that case the Court of Justice could interpret the Treaty and leave it to the Tariefcommissie to decide whether and how it would use the interpretation. However, by the time the Court of Justice issued its opinion in *Costa* v. *E.N.E.L.* the Italian Constitutional Court had already ruled that the Justice of the Peace had to apply the nationalization statute no matter what the meaning of the Treaty of Rome.

The case posed a dilemma for the Court of Justice. On the one hand it could not afford to let the position of the Constitutional Court go unchallenged. On the other hand it was difficult to see what the Court of Justice could say or do.

Advocate General Lagrange could find no solution at a Community level to the dilemma posed by the Constitutional Court. Although he suggested that the Court of Justice was not required to reject the questions put to it by the Justice of the Peace, since the Court had previously held that it would not inquire into the use to which its responses might be put by the referring national court and it was not up to the Court of Justice to speculate on the significance of the decision of the Constitutional Court, he could see only three alternatives to the claim that the national courts must apply a subsequent national statute. Either (1) the present law of the Member States permitted the national courts to carry out their obligations under the Treaty, (2) the national constitutions would have to be amended to give the courts the power to apply Community law rather than subsequent domestic legislation in conflict with the Treaty, or (3) the state would eventually have to withdraw from the Communities. All three alternatives were based on national solutions. While the question went to the very heart of the Communities' future existence, he did not believe that Community law could impose its own primacy over national law.

The Court of Justice was not as cautious as its Advocate General. In a legal *tour de force* it asserted that as a result of the pre-eminence of Community law over national law, "a subsequent unilateral act that would be incompatible with the Community concept cannot be asserted. Thus article

[37] The Italian Government also argued that the Justice of the Peace had requested the Court of Justice to declare whether the statute was in conflict with the Treaty which, it said, the Court of Justice could do only under the procedure of articles 169-171.

177 may be applied, notwithstanding any national law, where there is a question of Treaty interpretation."

Technically, all that the Court of Justice had decided was that it could respond to the questions which had been put to it by the Justice of the Peace. However, by basing its decision on the pre-eminence of Community law in a case arising in a national court, the Court of Justice had made it clear that the national courts are obligated to recognize the supremacy of Community law in the legal proceedings which come before them and to do all that is necessary to safeguard the rights of individuals under the Treaty, an obligation which includes the requirement that national courts of last resort refer prejudicial questions to the Court of Justice.[38]

Nevertheless, there is no procedure presently available by which the Court of Justice or any other Community institution can intervene in domestic litigation to require a national court to fulfill these obligations. Only articles 169-171 can be of any use, and their possibilities are limited. The main difficulty is that the procedure cannot be commenced until the Member State has failed to fulfill an obligation. In the case of litigation the failure of the courts to fulfill a Community obligation does not mature until there is a final judgment which is no longer subject to appeal or revision. As a result a judgment of the Court of Justice can have no effect on the case in the national court.

An action under articles 169-171 could focus on any one of three failures: (1) that of the state for having legislation in conflict with Community law, which is the usual failure alleged in an action under articles 169-171, (2) that of the national court of last resort for not requesting an interpretation of the Community law under article 177, or (3) that of the national court for not having safeguarded the rights of the individuals under Community law, presumably by refusing to recognize the supremacy of Community law. It has often been thought that the action would focus on the first of the three failures, the existence of national legislation in conflict with Community law. Although a decision of the Court of Justice that the national law was in conflict with the Community law would have no effect in the case already decided, it would serve as a form of appeal from the national judgment "in

[38] The Court of Justice interpreted the substantive articles in a manner such that the nationalization statute need not have been found in conflict with the Treaty. Nevertheless, on May 1, 1966 the Justice of the Peace of Milan held "inapplicable – in view of article 37 EEC Treaty and in view of the interpretation given by the Court of Justice in its judgment of July 15, 1964 – the Law No. 1643 of December 6, 1962 and the Presidential decrees rendered thereunder." EEC Document JUR/S/1944/66 quoted in Stein and Hay, Law and Institutions in the Atlantic Area 208-09 (1967). This decision of the Justice of the Peace has had no apparent effect on the validity of the nationalization save for the inability of E.N.E.L. to collect at least that one electric bill from Costa.

the interest of the law."[39] It would serve to determine whether the judgment in the national court was correct in its interpretation of Community law and on the relationship between Community law and the national law. Execution of an adverse judgment of the Court of Justice would require the repeal of the national legislation.

The *commissaire du gouvernement* in a case before the French Conseil d'État used the existence of this procedure as an argument that it was not necessary for the Conseil d'État to request an interpretation of Community law where one of the possible interpretations would have conflicted with a subsequent French law of some political importance.[40] She said that it was the duty of the Conseil d'État as a French administrative court to apply a French statute even if that statute was alleged to be "invalid" under either the Constitution or pre-existing Community law. In both cases, she argued, there are appropriate institutions to decide whether the statute is invalid and to draw the necessary conclusions. In the one case it is the Constitutional Council,[41] in the other it is the Court of Justice in a proceeding brought under articles 169-171.

This argument, based entirely on French concepts of the division of judicial responsibilities, caused a Dutch member of the European Parliament to ask the Commission why it has not begun the "difficult but inevitable" use of the procedure envisaged under articles 169-171 against the failure of the Conseil d'État to fulfill its obligations.[42] This question followed a series of questions three years before by the same Dutch member of the European Parliament which had been prompted by decisions of the French Conseil d'État and Cour de Cassation in which they had taken the responsibility unto themselves to rule that French law rather than Community law was applicable. In re-

[39] An appeal "in the interest of the law" is one which can be taken by the public officials for the purpose of establishing the correct interpretation of the law but only after the time for appeal by the litigants has expired. It has no effect on the outcome of the case as respects the litigants. Such a procedure is available in all the Member States except Germany, [1969-70] Eur. Parl. Docs., No. 94 at 25 (1969).

[40] Questiaux, conclusions in Syndicat général des fabricants de semoules en France, Conseil d'Etat, March 1, 1968, 57 Rev. Cr. D.I.P. 516, 525 (1968), [1970] Comm. Mkt. L. R. 395. Cf. Odent, *L'article 177 du Traité de Rome et la jurisprudence du Conseil d'Etat*, Bulletin de l'association des juristes européens 5, 16-17 (Nos. 23-24, 1965). See the discussion of the case in Chapter IV.

[41] The Constitutional Council may consider the constitutionality of a law only prior to its promulgation. The law may be referred to the Council by the President of the Republic, the Prime Minister or the President of either chamber of the Parliament. Once promulgated the law may no longer be subjected to constitutional attack. Constitution, art. 61. This authority to declare unconstitutional a law or a portion thereof was used for the first time in the decision of the Constitutional Council of July 16, 1971, D.S. 1972. Jur. 685, J.C.P. 1971. II. 16837. Beardsley, *The Constitutional Council and Constitutional Liberties in France*, 20 Am. J. Com. L. 431 (1972).

[42] Parliamentary Question 349/69, 13 E.E.C. J.O. C 20/3 (1970).

sponse the Commission had said that articles 169-171 were applicable to the actions of a "court of a Member State when it violates article 177 of the EEC Treaty" as well as to the actions of the national parliaments and governments when they violate Community law.[43]

In its current response the Commission affirmed that the use of articles 169-171 "must certainly not be excluded" where national courts have failed to fulfill their obligations.[44] However, it noted that after its 1967 reply the Legal Committee of the European Parliament had concluded that "the possible use of article 169 clashes ... with the independence of the judicial power vis-à-vis the executive power."[45] These considerations led the Commission "to think that the commencement of the procedure described in article 169 of the EEC Treaty must not be envisaged in all the cases where a decision of a national court misjudges the meaning of Community law."[46]

The hesitation of the European Parliament and the Commission is understandable, but it is misplaced. The Government of the Member State which lost a case under articles 169-171 would have no responsibility to pressure its courts to change their jurisprudence. The pressure is intended to come from the Court of Justice. There is nothing improper about such pressure. As mentioned above the proceedings under articles 169-171 would commence only after the final judgment in the national courts and would have no effect on the decision in that case. In effect such an action would be a Community equivalent of the standard action in international law for a "denial of justice" and would be intended to affect future actions of the national courts. Nevertheless, because of the hesitation of the Parliament and the Commission there is no procedure currently available by which the failure of the national courts to fulfill their Community obligations is subject to any control of the Court of Justice.

The obligations placed on the national courts by the Treaty of Rome and its interpretation by the Court of Justice are obligations which the national courts will themselves have to acknowledge if these obligations are to be fulfilled. However, before the national courts can be expected to engage in the "fruitful collaboration" with the Court of Justice called for by the European Parliament,[47] they will have to find that their obligations as national courts coincide with their obligations under Community law. So long as their obligations to the Community and to the nation are seen as conflicting with one another, the national courts will fulfill their obligations to the nation.

[43] Response to Parliamentary Question 100, 10 E.E.C. J.O. 270/2 (1967).
[44] Response to Parliamentary Question 349/69, 13 E.E.C. J.O. C 20/3 (1970).
[45] [1969-70] Eur. Parl. Doc., No. 94 at 24 (1969).
[46] Response to Parliamentary Question 349/69, 13 E.E.C. J.O. C 20/3)1970).
[47] Resolution of the European Parliament, October 8, 1969, 12 E.E.C. J.O. C 139/19 (1969).

They should not be criticized for this attitude. It is exactly the same attitude displayed by the Court of Justice in its sense of obligation to Community law. The national courts are part of the institutional structure of the Member States. They draw their authority from the state and their primary obligation is to the law of that state.

Nevertheless, the French courts in particular have been subjected to considerable criticism for their reluctance to use article 177. At least one prejudicial question had come from the courts of every other Member State prior to the first prejudicial question from a French court, that from the Court of Appeal of Colmar on June 1, 1965.[48] The French court about which the most concern has been expressed, the Conseil d'État, did not refer a prejudicial question until July 10, 1970.[49]

The concern has often been expressed that this reluctance on the part of the French courts to use the Community procedure was a result of feelings of nationalism greater than those of the courts of the other Member States. Perhaps that has been a factor, but another important factor has been that the history of the interpretation and application of treaties in the French courts has left them in a difficult position, both technically and politically, to apply Community law in a manner inconsistent with either a subsequent French statute or the political judgment of the Government. Therefore, the prospects for the future of Community law in the French courts can be understood only in the light of the study of that history.

[48] La Hessische Knappschaft v. Maison Singer, Cour d'appel de Colmar, June 1, 1965, J.C.P. 1966. II. 14578 (2e espèce), Gaz. Pal. 1965. 2. 102.

[49] Syndicat national du commerce extérieur des céréales, Conseil d'Etat, July 10, 1970, J.C.P. 1971. II. 16701 (concl. Questiaux, note Ruzié), 6 Rev. Tr. Dr. Eur. 742 (concl. Questiaux) (1970).

CHAPTER II

TREATIES IN THE CONSEIL D'ÉTAT

THE ORGANIZATIONAL CONTEXT

The courts were among the many institutions which lost both power and prestige in the French Revolution. The pre-Revolutionary courts were important and powerful forces in France. Unfortunately, they became one of the main institutions into which the nobility retreated. As such they became a bastion of the forces of privilege, local power, and the status quo against the royal desires for modernization and centralization. The eighteenth century was one of constant turmoil in the relations between the crown and the courts, turmoil which reached its height during the temporary banishment of the Parlement of Paris at the end of the reign of Louis XV[1] and the forced registration of Turgot's decrees in 1776 by Louis XVI at a formal *lit de justice*.[2]

If the conflict had merely been one between an embattled landed aristocracy and a centralizing monarchy, it might not have had the adverse impact on the post-Revolutionary French courts which in fact it had. But by the time of the Revolution the resistance to the King, which had previously received the support of the general population as a protection of liberties against centralized power, was seen to have been a resistance to the new liberal economic and political ideas of the emerging bourgeoisie. As a result the courts suffered a drastic loss of power in the new organization of the state.

The fundamental principle on which the state was organized following 1789 was the doctrine of the separation of powers between the three branches of government as described by Montesquieu. Henceforth, there would be a legislature to enact the laws, an executive to administer them and courts to adjudicate the disputes which arose under them. The three branches of government each had their area of competence and none of them would

[1] Shennan, The Parlement of Paris 284-325 (1968).

[2] The decree abolishing the guilds and corporations is found in 23 Isambert, Anciennes Lois Françaises 370 (1826) and in translation in Shepherd, Turgot and the Six Edicts 182 (1903). The decree reinstating them is found in 24 Isambert, Anciennes Lois Françaises at 74.

intrude on the other two. Unfortunately for the symmetry of the theory on which the state was organized, in almost every French constitution since 1789 the legislative and executive branches of government have alternated in dominating the state.

The relative position of the courts has shown more continuity. The courts were placed in a subordinate position at the time of the Revolution and that subordinate position has not changed from constitution to constitution. One of the first acts of the Revolution was to abolish the existing court system and to replace it with a new one by the decree of August 16-24, 1790.[3] The new court system was placed under many restrictions so as to be sure that it would not interfere with the reforms which were taking place. The particular restriction which most influenced the development of the law in respect to treaties is the same which led to the creation of the Conseil d'État as an administrative tribunal. The courts were prohibited from interfering in any manner with the operations of the administration.[4]

The prohibition placed on the courts in 1790 against interfering with the operations of the administration was understood to prohibit them from considering complaints against the state or its officers. Individuals who felt aggrieved by an official action could appeal to the official whose action was in question and to his hierarchical superiors. As a result of the general dissatisfaction with this system, when the Conseil d'État was organized in 1799, one of the tasks to which it was assigned was that of advising the Consuls, the Government of the time, on disputes with private individuals in which the administration had ruled adversely on the complaint.[5]

In the reorganization of the Conseil d'État in 1806 the Section du contentieux was created to specialize in the consideration of complaints against the state and a formalized procedure was established.[6] This is usually considered to mark the beginning of the Conseil d'État as a court. However, even in its judicial capacity it continued to act merely as an advisor to the Emperor. It did not decide cases in its own name but prepared a decree for his signature. In 1806 this system of "retained justice," i.e., justice retained by the Emperor, did not weaken the Conseil d'État in its judicial capacity. The Conseil d'État was the Emperor's main advisor in all matters of law and

[3] S. 1789-1830. L. 49.

[4] Title II, art. 13. "The judicial functions are distinct and will always remain separated from the administrative functions. Under penalty of forfeiture the judges cannot trouble in any manner whatsoever the operations of the administrative corps nor cite before them administrators for reasons arising out of their duties."

[5] Règlement of 5 niv. an 8 (Dec. 26, 1799), art. 11, S. 1799-1830. L. 522, 12 D. Rép. 179.

[6] Decree of June 11, 1806, S. 1789-1830. L. 719, 12 D. Rép. 180.

of administration. There was little reason to expect its advice to be rejected in respect to individual complaints against the state.

The fall of the Empire and the Restoration of the Bourbons to the throne of France left the Conseil d'État in a particularly exposed position. Although its proven utility required its retention, it was distrusted as an innovation of the hated imperial regime. As the central institution in the administration of the state, it was potentially extremely powerful, too powerful for the liking of the Government. This distrust of the Conseil d'État was modified only in part by the replacement of a major portion of its membership with men who were considered to be more trustworthy, a cleansing process which was to reoccur after subsequent changes of regime.[7] The Conseil d'État quickly learned the value of restricting its role, both as an advisor and as a "court", to the efficient administration of the state, a role it can play under any regime.

From 1815 to 1872 the foundation was laid for the effective control of administrative action. Not only could the Conseil d'État recommend the award of money damages against the state, but it could recommend the annulment of illegal administrative acts. This was one of the benefits of acting as an advisor to the crown rather than as an independent court. In theory it was the King or Emperor who annulled the offending act. Even so the Conseil d'État developed this power slowly and carefully. While at first it only recommended the annulment of individual administrative acts, by mid-century it had asserted its power over some forms of regulations.[8]

ACT OF GOVERNMENT

The price paid for this increasing power over administrative acts was a self-imposed limitation over Acts of Government and their implementation.[9] Although the definition of an Act of Government has changed over time, its primary characteristic has remained constant. The administrative courts cannot consider the legality of an Act of Government even though the act otherwise meets all the formal criteria for adjudication. In many respects the concept of the Act of Government serves the same function as does the concept of the political question in the United States.

The political nature of the Act of Government has been evident since the

[7] See generally, Leonardi, Le Conseil d'Etat sous la Restoration (1909). In 1830, 20 of the 38 members of the Conseil d'Etat were dismissed. 2 Cobban, A History of Modern France 95 (2nd ed. 1965).

[8] In his conclusions in Chemins de fer du Nord, Conseil d'Etat, Dec. 6, 1907, D.P. 1909. 3. 57, S. 1908. 3. 1, the *commissaire du gouvernement* Tardieu set the beginning date for the competence of the Conseil d'Etat over most regulations at "about 1842." In a note to the same case in 25 Rev. Dr. Pub. 38, 41 (1908), Jèze set the date at 1845.

[9] Hauriou, Précis de droit administratif et de droit public 435 (10e éd. 1921).

earliest important cases, all of which involved the claims of the former imperial family or their transferees for benefits granted during the First Empire.[10] These claims were an offense to the Restoration, the official theory of which was that Louis XVIII had rightfully been king since the death of his brother and nephew in 1793. The Empire was viewed as merely the last of the usurper governments to deprive him of the enjoyment of the throne. The claims were denied on the grounds that the Conseil d'État lacked jurisdiction over the case, with one exception which was denied on the merits.[11] Although the political nature of the decisions was obvious, the majority of the opinions simply stated the result and gave no reasons therefore.

Several of the claims of the imperial family were based on treaties, which naturally led to the conclusion that those treaties were not subject to the jurisdiction of the Conseil d'État.[12] Other early treaty cases did not have the same emotional content as those involving the claims of the imperial family, but several of them involved the foreign policy of France at a rather high level. The disposition of these cases set the stage for the manner in which treaties were considered, or more often not considered, by the Conseil d'État for the next hundred years.

Two cases which illustrate the attitude of the Conseil d'État arose out of a secret agreement with Algeria by which certain named ships were not subject to the blockade of England declared by the decree of Berlin of November 21, 1806.[13] When several of these ships were taken by French privateers, the owners protested the action of the prize court. In one of the cases the prize court condemned the ship without knowledge of the agreement. The Conseil d'État reversed the decision on the ground that privateers are bound by treaties with foreign states.[14] In another case the proceeds from the condemnation of the ship were turned over to the French consul in Algiers. When the privateer brought an action to have the money turned over to him, the

[10] Dame de Beauharnais, Duchesse de Saint-Leu, Conseil, d'État, Dec. 5, 1838, S. 1839. 2. 552, 10 D. Rép. 438; Murat, Comtesse de Lipona, Conseil d'État, July 23, 1823, S. 1822-24. 2. 246, Jour. Pal. J.A. 1820-24. 688; Fain v. Min. des Finances, Conseil d'État, Jan. 22, 1823, S. 1822-24. 2. 162, Jour. Pal. J.A. 1820-24. 586; Laffitte, Conseil d'État, May 1, 1822, S. 1822-24. 2. 63, Jour. Pal. J.A. 1820-24. 436. *Murat* involved a claim of title to specific real estate. The other cases involved claims for money.

[11] Perret, Conseil d'État, Dec. 5, 1833, S. 1834. 2. 630, 42 D. Rép. 557.

[12] Murat, Comtesse de Lipona, Conseil d'État, July 23, 1823, S. 1822-24. 2. 246, Jour. Pal. J.A. 1820-24. 688; Fain v. Min. des Finances, Conseil d'État, Jan. 22, 1823, S. 1822-24. 2. 162, Jour. Pal. J.A. 1820-24. 586. *Contra*, Perret, Conseil d'État, Dec. 5, 1833, S. 1834. 2. 630, 42 D. Rép. 557.

[13] S. 1789-1830. L. 737.

[14] Bacri v. Le Brave, Conseil d'État, July 17, 1816, S. 1815-18. 2. 174, Jour. Pal. J.A. 1814-19. 241.

Conseil d'État refused saying that it was not competent to judge questions relative to the execution of treaties.[15]

The pattern established by these two cases continued throughout the handful of treaty cases in the Conseil d'État prior to 1872.[16] The Conseil d'État would not accept jurisdiction on the complaint of a private party either to enforce a treaty against the Government or to enforce some other rule in the face of a conflicting treaty. However, it would recognize the existence of a treaty when that was necessary in order to uphold the action of the Government in the face of otherwise applicable rules.

During the Second Empire that which had been implicit in the earlier decisions involving treaties or the imperial family became explicit. The Conseil d'État would refuse to consider cases in which the action of the Government had been taken for reasons of "high politics".

An act of high politics was said to be no longer in the legal realm but constituted an act of sovereignty which could not be submitted to the consideration of a judicial body.[17] Affirmed many times during the twenty years of the Second Empire, the most striking application of this doctrine was the refusal of the Conseil d'État to consider the legality of the seizure of a book written by the Duc d'Aumale, a son of the deposed king, Louis-Phillippe.[18] The *commissaire du gouvernement* pointed out that this was not an ordinary seizure of a book, an act which could happen to any citizen. The Government saw the book as an indirect call for the replacement of the Second Empire by a new Orléanist monarchy. Since the motives for the seizure of the book were of a political nature in the highest degree, they could not be questioned before the Conseil d'État.

The attitude towards the Act of Government began to change soon after a new statute of the Conseil d'État was enacted in 1872 upon the fall of the Second Empire and the creation of the Third Republic.[19] The most impor-

[15] Lecosani v. Le Chasseur, Conseil d'État, June 17, 1820, S. 1819-21. 2. 274, Jour. Pal. J.A. 1820-24. 76.

[16] A list of thirteen cases is given in Favoreu, Du déni de justice en droit public français 206n (1964). Other than the cases involving the former imperial family, cited above, none of these cases appear to have had any particular political significance. The claims were mostly for money alleged to be due either under the terms of treaty, for compensation for the loss of property or monopolies as a result of a treaty or because of an allegedly incorrect partition among the private beneficiaries of indemnities paid to France by a foreign government.

[17] See Note to Famille d'Orléans, Conseil d'État, June 18, 1852, D.P. 1852. 3. 17.

[18] Duc d'Aumale, Conseil d'État, May 9, 1867, D.P. 1867. 3. 49 (concl. Aucoc), S. 1867. 2. 124 (concl. Aucoc). Cf. le Courrier du Dimanche, Conseil d'État, Aug. 14, 1865, D.P. 1866. 3. 17 (concl. Faré), S. 1866. 2. 132 (concl. Faré), in which the Conseil d'État exercised jurisdiction over the suspension of the newspaper and la Gazette de France, Conseil d'État, May 31, 1866, D.P. 1866. 3. 65 (concl. Hôpital), S. 1867. 2. 244, in which it exercised jurisdiction over a warning prior to suspension.

[19] Law of May 24, 1872, D.P. 1872. 4. 88, S. 1871-75. L. 210.

tant reform brought about by the new statute was the abolition of the "retained justice," by which the Conseil d'État had prepared a decree for the signature of the Emperor, in favor of a "delegated justice." Beginning in 1872 the Conseil d'État has decided in its own name the cases which come before it. In one sense this formal change may have been of little significance. Such records as exist indicate that from 1806 to 1871 the recommendations of the Conseil d'État had been rejected only two or three times, and on those occasions the King or Emperor had insisted upon a more favorable result for the private claimant.[20] However, it is easy to believe that the knowledge that the King or Emperor would have to sign the decree was an inhibition on judicial independence in cases of political significance. More importantly, it was not in keeping with the new republican form of government for a court dispensing justice to allow the state to violate the law merely because the Government had political reasons to do so.

The redefinition of the Act of Government first occurred in 1875 in another case involving the imperial family, this time the family of the Emperor Louis-Napoléon, who had so recently abdicated.[21] In 1853 the Emperor had named his cousin, Prince Napoléon-Joseph Bonaparte, as a Lieutenant-General of the Armies. The 1873 military annual, the first to appear after the fall of the Second Empire, failed to list the Prince as an army officer. He inquired whether the omission was inadvertent or deliberate and, on being told it was deliberate, formally requested his reinstatement on the list. The refusal of the Minister of War gave rise to an action in the Conseil d'État since the rights of an officer were determined by his position on the list in the annual, rights which were regarded as property rights of the individual officer.[22]

The Minister of War denied the competence of the Conseil d'État to hear the case on the grounds that the decision not to list the Prince as a Lieutenant-General had been made by the Council of Ministers and the subsequent refusal to reinstate him was in execution of that decision. The Minister claimed that the political nature of the decision made it an Act of Government not subject to review.

By deciding the case for the Government on the merits the Conseil d'État implicitly accepted the two aspects of the argument presented to it by its *commissaire du gouvernement* David. The first was that the Conseil d'État had the authority to decide whether an act was or was not an Act of Government.

[20] Waline, Droit administratif ¶ 40 (9e éd. 1963).

[21] Prince Napoléon, Conseil d'État, Feb. 19, 1875, D.P. 1875. 3. 18 (concl. David), S. 1875. 2. 95.

[22] Hounau, Conseil d'État, Feb. 6, 1874, D.P. 1875. 3. 17, S. 1876. 2. 26.

It was not obligated to accept the Government's characterization. It is not clear whether this was a change from prior theory, but it was certainly a change in practice. There is no indication that the Conseil d'État had ever previously made an independent judgment of its authority to consider a case on the merits once the Government alleged that it involved an Act of Government. Secondly, the Conseil d'État rejected its prior holdings that a decision made by the Council of Ministers or dictated by a political motive was by that very fact an Act of Government.

The decision in *Prince Napoléon* was enthusiastically welcomed for, as was said a few years later by the *commissaire du gouvernement* Gomel in one of the many cases before the Tribunal des Conflits involving the expulsion of the Jesuits, if the "political motive" for which an action was taken was sufficient to determine that it was an Act of Government, "it would be enough for the administration to proclaim that any interference that it brings to the liberty or property of this or that class of citizens is a measure of high policy in order for the citizens thus injured in the rights assured to them by the laws to be deprived of every means of recourse."[23]

Prince Napoléon was only one of a long line of cases in which the Conseil d'État, now speaking in its own name, extended the range and effectiveness of its jurisdiction. While it continues to exercise its concern for efficient administration, it has also become the primary protector of the rights of the individual against organized society. Among the more important monuments of this slow development are the creation of the action for misuse of power as a grounds for striking down an otherwise valid administrative act;[24] the recognition of the general jurisdiction of the Conseil d'État in matters of administrative law;[25] the extension of standing to sue beyond those with a direct and exclusive personal interest;[26] and in 1907 the extension of the action for annulment to all general regulations, including the *règlements d'administration publique*, regulations which can be adopted only after prior consultation with the appropriate committee of the Conseil d'État itself.[27] Following the 1907 decision the Conseil d'État was competent over almost

[23] Gomel, Conclusions in Bouffier v. Fache, Tribunal des Conflits, Nov. 5, 1880, D.P. 1880. 3. 128.

[24] Pariset, Conseil d'État, Nov. 26, 1875, D.P. 1876. 3. 41.

[25] Cadot, Conseil d'État, Dec. 13, 1889, D.P. 1891. 3. 41 (concl. Jagerschmidt), S. 1892. 3. 17 (note Hauriou).

[26] Casanova, Conseil d'État, March 29, 1901, D.P. 1902. 3. 34, S. 1901. 3. 73 (note Hauriou).

[27] Chemins de fer de l'Est. Conseil d'État, Dec. 6, 1907, D.P. 1909. 3. 57 (concl. Tardieu), S. 1908. 3. 1 (note Hauriou, concl. Tardieu), 25 Rev. Dr. Pub. 38 (note Jèze) (1908).

all actions taken by the executive whether those actions were individual or general, unless the action was an Act of Government.[28]

In the light of these later developments extending the rule of law in administrative matters there has been some feeling that the Act of Government has no place in a republican regime. No matter what the arguments for its retention it is too similar to the "reasons of state" which became discredited from overuse and it is a denial of the basic concept of government under law. However, in spite of these arguments, the concept of the Act of Government has been retained. Its retention is justified on political grounds and is supported by legal text.

The political considerations have been of four varieties. The first arose out of the fact that the republican regime was at least as much in danger of being overthrown by partisans of the various royal and imperial families as had been any previous regime. It was thought that the Government had to be given sufficient freedom to deal with the threat. The threat to the regime did not disappear when the royalist movement faded into obscurity fifty to sixty years ago. Internal or external military action has led to three changes of Government and one abortive coup since 1940.

The second consideration was simply that France was not yet ready to turn over to a court the responsibility of protecting it from the political branches of government. To do so, it was feared, would turn France from a parliamentary regime into a regime of the courts.[29] This concern appears time and time again to limit the jurisdiction of the courts in respect to matters which have political overtones.

A third consideration of particular relevance to the field of foreign affairs is that an untoward decision might interfere unduly with the Government's foreign policy. While this is a concern which can easily be carried to an extreme, it is not one which can be ignored.[30]

[28] Other than those acts which are denominated Acts of Government, the executive can currently take no actions which are not subject to the control of the Conseil d'État. However, it is still recognized that actions of provisional governments before the regular institutions of the state have been re-established, such as those taken in 1848, 1851, 1870 and under art. 92 of the Constitution of 1958, are also free from the control of the Conseil d'État. Favoreu, Déni de justice 131-56; Brown, *De Gaulle's Republic and the Rule of Law Judicial Review and the Conseil d'État*, 46 B. U. L. Rev. 462 (1966).

[29] Rivero, *Le juge administratif français· un juge qui gouvern?*, D. 1951. chron. 21. For a similar reaction in respect to the European Communities see J.-P. Colin, Le Gouvernement des juges dans les Communautés Européennes (1966) and in respect to the United States see Lambert, Le gouvernement des juges et la lutte contre la législation sociale aux États-Unis (1921).

[30] At the time that France placed an embargo on the shipment of military aircraft to Israel in January 1969 and refused to repay Israel the downpayment the Minister of Defense stated that the decision was an Act of Government which the French courts had traditionally considered outside their jurisdiction. *Le Monde* (Paris), Jan. 11, 1969, p. 3.

The fourth consideration was the least attractive and has been often rejected as a justification for the continuation of the Act of Government, howevermuch it may bean adequate explanation. Even though the new regime was republican and presumably committed to the rule of law, the Conseil d'État has been constantly forced to consider its political relationship with the Government and to trim its sails when the going got too rough. One way of doing this has been to deny its jurisdiction over particular acts of importance to the Government.[31]

The textual argument arose out of articles 9 and 26 of the law of May 24, 1872 which had reorganized the Conseil d'État.[32] Article 9 provided that "The Conseil d'État decides in last resort on complaints in matters of *administrative* litigation...." [Emphasis added.] While the Conseil d'État obviously has the primary responsibility to determine whether the question presented to it is administrative, the last word rests with the Tribunal des Conflits. The major function of this court, which is presided over by the Minister of Justice and whose members come from the Conseil d'État and the Cour de Cassation, is to decide on the conflicts of jurisdiction between the administrative authorities and administrative tribunals on the one hand and the criminal and civil courts on the other.[33] In addition article 26 specified that Ministers can bring before the Tribunal des Conflits those cases in which they claim that the Conseil d'État has exceeded its jurisdiction, i.e. has taken jurisdiction of a case which is not administrative.[34] The conclusion drawn from these two provisions was that if there were acts of the executive which were not administrative and could not, therefore, be considered by the Conseil d'État, those acts must be Acts of Government. The only question left was how to determine which acts fit this description.

In *Prince Napoléon* the *commissaire du gouvernement* David defined Acts of Government as those acts the "objects for which the law thought it necessary to confer general powers on the Government to which it has virtually

[31] One member of the Conseil d'État has remarked that "it was ... impossible for the [Conseil d'État] to contradict the express provisions of the laws of Vichy. Such decisions would not have failed to bring about the publication of a law suppressing all jurisdiction in the matter." Bouffandeau, *Le juge de l'excès de pouvoir jusqu'à la Libération du territoire métropolitain*, Conseil d'État: Etudes et Documents 23 (1947), as quoted in Favoreu, Déni de justice 140. See also text at note 98 *infra* and following.

[32] D.P. 1872. 4. 88, S. 1871-75. L. 210. 1 Odent, Cours de contentieux administratif, 1965-66 at 205. This result was not dictated by either the language or the legislative history of arts. 9 and 26. Mignon, *Une emprise nouvelle du principe de légalité: Les actes de gouvernement*, D. 1951. chron. 53.

[33] Art. 25.

[34] Ironically, the Government has never brought a matter to the Tribunal des Conflits in which it alleged that the Conseil d'État was improperly considering an Act of Government. 1 Odent, Contentieux administratif, 1965-66 at 443.

subordinated the individual rights of citizens in the superior interest of the state."[35] The list of such acts was limited in his view to those discretionary powers which the Government has (1) from the constitutional laws, when they exist, for the regulation and execution of diplomatic conventions, (2) from the laws concerning the police power and especially those relating to martial law, and (3) from the extraordinary laws designed to protect the regime against the anticipated attempts to regain power by the princes belonging to the former royal families.

David's definition confused two distinct ideas, discretionary acts, which can be brought before the Conseil d'État in its judicial capacity but over which it has limited control on the merits, and Acts of Government, which may not even be properly brought to its attention. While the result in both cases is a dismissal of the complaint brought against the actions of the the state, the distinction is useful. If an act is discretionary, there is presumably some text or doctrine of law which describes this act or category of acts, charges some person or persons with the exercise of the discretion, and places some limits on the manner and the extent to which the discretion is to be exercised. On the other hand the significance of the Act of Government is that the Conseil d'État is unwilling to consider whether any standards exist by which the discretionary acts can be limited.[36]

However, the recognition of the Conseil d'État as the body charged with the determination whether an act was an Act of Government gave room for further change in the doctrine, and the emphasis on a pre-existing legislative text gave the Conseil d'État the basis on which to make the judgment. This was illustrated some twelve years later when the Conseil d'État held that the dismissal of members of the Orléans and Murat families as army officers was a non-discretionary administrative act pursuant to the law of June 22, 1886 governing the status of the former ruling families of France.[37] As a result, the Conseil d'État had jurisdiction to consider whether their dismissal as army officers conformed to the statute. The Conseil d'État went on to interpret the statute in such a way as not to apply to the Murat family and, therefore, it annulled as to them the action of the Minister of War by which they had been dismissed.

Other authorities have given other criteria by which to determine which acts are Acts of Government. One attempt was to segregate those actions

[35] D.P. 1875. 3. at 19.
[36] Duez, Les Actes de gouvernement 22.
[37] Orléans, Conseil d'État, May 20, 1887, D.P. 1888. 3. 105 (concl. Marguerie), S. 1889. 3. 19 (concl. Marguerie); Murat, Conseil d'État, May 20, 1887, *ibid.*

which are by their nature administrative, over which the Conseil d'État has jurisdiction, from those actions which are by their nature governmental, over which it has no jurisdiction.[38] Another explanation which has been offered is that an Act of Government is a "mixed act undertaken by the Government either (1) in partnership with a non-administrative institution such as the Parliament or the courts, or (2) with a foreign government, or (3) which is inseparable from such an act."[39] Others deny that "mixed acts" are even properly called Acts of Government, much less seen as the prototype.[40]

In the face of this difficulty of defining the Act of Government some commentators have concluded that no adequate definition can be formulated; the examples can only be listed. There are various acts the legality of which the Conseil d'État will not review for various reasons.[41] If this is confusing the criterion with the result, it is because the real criteria are extra-legal and unique to some degree in respect to each type of Act of Government.

Other commentators have concluded that with the lack of a simple unifying criterion there is no such thing as an Act of Government.[42] Giving it a label implies the consistency of a doctrine. But all that exists is the denial of jurisdiction for a series of separate and unrelated causes. Unfortunately for the theory that no such doctrine as the Act of Government exists both the Tribunal des Conflits and the Conseil d'État have recently specifically used the words "Acts of Government."[43] They have thereby confirmed the existence of the doctrine, though without explaining the criteria by which such Acts can be recognized.

APPLICATION OF TREATIES AS LAW

It is not important for our purposes to resolve the doctrinal dispute over the proper definition of an Act of Government. What is important is that foreign affairs in general and treaties in particular have traditionally been included, thereby denoting that they could not be the subject matter of litigation in the Conseil d'État. With this as a starting point it was a long process before

[38] 2 Laferrière, Traité de la juridiction administrative et des recours contentieux 32 (2e éd. 1896); Chapus, *L'acte de gouvernement, monstre ou victime?*, D. 1958.chron. 5.

[39] Celier, conclusions in Gombert, Conseil d'État, March 28, 1947. S. 1947. 3. 89.

[40] Virally, *L'introuvable "acte de gouvernement"*, 68 Rev. Dr. Pub 317, 337-40 (1952).

[41] 1 de Laubadère, Traité elémentaire de droit administratif ¶ 416 (4e éd. 1967); Hauriou, Droit administratif 433.

[42] 1 Odent, Cour de contentieux administratif, 1949-50 at 68, cited by Waline, Droit administratif 218; Virally, *L'introuvable acte de gouvernement*, 68 Rev. Dr. Pub. 317 (1952). Odent no longer held this position by the time he taught his 1965-66 version of the course. See 1 Contentieux administratif, 1965-66 at 204.

[43] Rubin de Servens, Conseil d'État, March 2, 1962, D. 1962. Jur. 307, S. 1962. Jur. 147 (note Bourdoncle); Barbaran, Tribunal des Conflits, June 24, 1954, Rec. Cons. d'Ét. 1954. 712, S. 1955. 3. 6.

treaties were given the status of law in the Conseil d'État and even today they constitute a very special and restricted form of "law".

This does not mean that treaties created no effective rights or obligations for individuals in their relations with the state. France is bound by public international law to apply all treaties which it has ratified. As a routine matter treaties are implemented in the appropriate manner. Individuals have been the beneficiaries of this duty owed to the foreign state whether or not they have had a personal right to enforce the treaty in the Counseil d'État against the French state.[44] If a treaty has been inadvertently overlooked or innocently misapplied, an administrative appeal has normally rectified the matter. When there are major difficulties the foreign state may intervene. Therefore, as a practical matter it can be said that the majority of treaties have always created effective rights for individuals in their relations with the state.

These techniques have not resolved all the problems. Foreign governments do not and cannot get involved in each and every dispute over the implementation or interpretation of a treaty. Nor if they did, would they always be able to resolve the dispute to the satisfaction of both states, much less to that of the individuals concerned. There will be cases in which individuals can get no satisfaction through appeal to diplomatic channels or to the administrative hierarchy. Their relief, if any, must come from the Conseil d'État.

It was not surprising in the early nineteenth century when the Conseil d'État was new and politically weak and France was beset with enemies on all sides that activities concerned with foreign affairs would be considered Acts of Government outside the scope of review. However, once the Conseil d'État had solidified its position and was actively extending its competence into previously forbidden domestic areas, it was considered intolerable for diplomatic agents to claim in all cases the ancient "reasons of state" which were allowed less and less often in domestic matters.[45]

This was especially so because many of the cases could have only internal effects and were of little or no interest to the foreign government. One of the more striking examples involving treaties was the refusal of the Conseil d'État to review the disposition to the private claimants of a lump sum claims settlement with a foreign state.[46] It was hard to see in most cases why the foreign

[44] This is illustrated by the cases cited above in which the French Government applied the secret agreement with Algeria that certain named ships were not subject to the French blockade of Great Britain in such a manner as to protect the owners of those ships.

[45] Jèze, note to Bachatou, Conseil d'État, Feb. 12, 1904, 21 Rev. Dr. Pub. 78 (1904).

[46] Legrand, Conseil d'État, Feb. 12, 1870, D.P. 1870. 3. 72; Dubois, Conseil d'État, April 30, 1867, D.P. 1868. 3. 28, S. 1867. 2. 299; Dussaud, Conseil d'État, Dec. 7, 1843, S. 1844. 2. 136 (note Devill).

government would be concerned which private claimants, if any, received the payment from the French Government once the debt had been discharged to France. This was demonstrated by the fact that in 1870 the Cour de Cassation held that the ordinary courts could determine which heirs a Franco-Mexican claims commission intended when it made an award to the "representatives" of a Frenchman killed in Mexico in 1857.[47]

There were a few isolated instances in which the Conseil d'État would adjudicate matters involving treaties. One involved the taxation of consuls. Immediately after the Revolution the Ministry of Foreign Affairs had directed that as a matter of international custom foreign consuls were free of taxation in France on a reciprocal basis to the same extent that French consuls were free from taxation in the other country.[48] There was never any question of the jurisdiction of the Counseil d'État to consider complaints brought by the consul against local tax officials who, it was alleged, had violated the directions of the Ministry of Foreign Affairs.[49] This was so even though the dispute posed a question of international law and usually required the Conseil d'État to ask the Ministry of Foreign Affairs the extent to which reciprocity was granted in the other country.

As time went on this international custom of the immunity of consuls from taxation on a basis of reciprocity was incorporated in a number of bilateral consular conventions. The Conseil d'État continued to adjudicate the cases, relying on the interpretation of the conventions given by the Minister of Foreign Affairs as they had earlier relied upon his statement of the applicable international custom.[50]

Then, in 1901 and 1907 the unexpected occurred, the Conseil d'État interpreted the consular convention with Chile in a manner contrary to the interpretation given by the Minister of Foreign Affairs.[51] At the time no one seems to have seen these decisions as affecting the law regarding the role of treaties in the Conseil d'État; they were seen as having to do only with the law of the taxation of consuls.

There was also a 1913 case in which a treaty involving the international shipment of parcel post was interpreted in a manner contrary to that of the

[47] Delarbre v. Chédeville, Cass. req., Aug. 16, 1870, D.P. 1871. 1. 279, S. 1871. 1. 20.

[48] 12 D. Rép. 281.

[49] Vereker, Conseil d'État, Jan. 28, 1881, D.P. 1882. 3. 54, S. 1882. 3. 40; Wesphal Castelnau, Conseil d'État, Sept. 7, 1848, D.P. 1849. 3. 2, S. 1849. 2. 59; Ullern, Conseil d'État, Nov. 17, 1843, D.P. 1844. 3. 42, S. 1844. 2. 135.

[50] Saurer, Conseil d'État, May 21, 1926, D.H. 1926. 367, 54 Clunet 122 (1927); Rodrigo, Conseil d'État, June 11, 1920, Rec. Cons. d'Ét. 1920. 571, 24 Rev. Dr. Int'l. Pr. 310 (1921).

[51] Comolet, Conseil d'État, Jan. 23, 1907, D.P. 1909. 5. 59, 5 Rev. Dr. Int'l. Pr. 204 (1909); Ducaud, Conseil d'État, June 12, 1901, D.P. 1902. 3. 113, S. 1904. 3. 46.

postal authorities.[52] The case was not generally noticed until it was overruled twenty-two years later.[53] The fact that the Conseil d'État would decide the case can be explained on at least two grounds. The first is that the defendant was a privately owned railroad rather than the state. This explanation implies the recognition of the distinction long present in the Cour de Cassation between those disputes over treaties which concern only private matters and those which raise questions of public order.

The second, and more likely possibility, arises out of the fact that the Conseil d'État is the forum which adjudicates disputes involving the international shipment of parcel post.[54] Since this is true, it was all but impossible for the Conseil d'État not to turn to the treaty for the applicable substantive rule. An obvious result, and yet it was contrary to the prevailing doctrine.

These cases established no precedent in respect to treaties in general. They are significant only as a demonstration that the Conseil d'État could not continue to live with its often professed lack of competence to apply treaties.[55]

The lack of competence in the Conseil d'État had always been understood to extend to the administrative acts by which an Act of Government was implemented as well as to the Act of Government itself. This was obvious in the context of the cases involving the former ruling families. The refusal of some administrative official to pay a claim was so intimately tied to the Governmental decision that the exercise of jurisdiction over the act – or refusal to act – of the administrative official would have in fact been the exercise of jurisdiction over the governmental decision itself. Therefore, administrative acts implementing Acts of Government were said to be themselves Acts of Government.

While this result was obvious when the Act of Government and the implementing act were as intimately tied together as they were in the cases involving the former ruling families, it became less so as the administrative act in question became more detached from the Act of Government. The problem exists whenever there is an Act of Government,[56] but it is most acute

[52] Chemins de fer de l'Est, Conseil d'État, Feb. 28, 1913, Rec. Cons. d'Ét. 1913. 307.

[53] Chemins de fer du Nord, Conseil d'État, July 27, 1935, S. 1936. 3. 83, Gaz. Pal. 1935. 2. 553.

[54] J.-D. Ricard, *Aux sources de la compétence juridictionnelle en matière de colis postaux*, D.H. 1937. chron. 13.

[55] Other isolated cases have been cited in de la Pradelle, *Juridiction administrative et droit international*, 16 Conseil d'État: Etudes et Documents 13, 20 (1962) and in Rousseau, Principes généraux du droit international public ¶ 415 (1944). In many of the cases cited the Conseil d'État applied the treaty to deny its competence in the matter. These were not good precedents for the use of a treaty affirmatively against the state.

[56] In Dejean, Conseil d'État, May 6, 1970, 87 Rev. Dr. Pub. 533 (1971), a letter written by an administrative official to a criminal court in respect to the validity of a construction permit was detachable from the criminal process and was, therefore, subject to the jurisdiction of the Conseil d'État.

in respect to treaties. This is so partly because treaties are increasingly used to legislate on matters of direct concern to private individuals, but also because they often require two levels of implementing acts. The first level consists of a general implementing act, typically in the form of a decree or regulation, providing the details for the application of the treaty in France. The second level consists of the application of the general implementing act to the individual.

As a result an individual might have three possible complaints: (1) the general implementing act was not in conformity with the treaty, (2) the individual implementing act was not in conformity with the treaty, (3) the individual implementing act was not in conformity with the general implementing act. A strict application of the Act of Government precluded the Conseil d'État from considering any one of these cases.

The change in doctrine which began in the 1920s commenced with the third of these possibilities, the non-conformity of the individual implementing act with the general implementing act. The problem was consciously faced for the first time in 1924.[57]

Article 68 of the Treaty of Versailles provided that products from the recovered portions of Alsace and Lorraine would enter Germany duty free for a period of five years.[58] Article 68 went on to say that "the French Government reserves the right to determine each year, by a decree to be notified to the German Government, the nature and quantity of the products which will benefit from this [duty free] franchise." The decree adopted for the year 1922 pursuant to the treaty governed the mechanism for determining which merchants qualified for the privilege of exporting duty free to Germany in addition to determining the nature and quality of the products covered by the franchise.

The complainants alleged that the provisions of this decree had been improperly applied to them. They had been denied the necessary authorization because of an attempted fraud on their part but, they claimed, the decree spoke only of successful frauds.

If prior practice had been followed, the complaint would have been dismissed for lack of jurisdiction as was requested by the state. However, the Conseil d'État held that "the measures to be taken by the French Govern-

[57] Goldschmidt, Conseil d'État, June 27, 1924, Rec. Cons. d'Ét. 1924. 607. The earlier decision of Bordj, Conseil d'État, July 16, 1920, Rec. Cons. d'Ét. 1920. 706, was cited by Laroque in a note to Min. des travaux publics v. Duhamel, Conseil d'État, Oct. 26, 1934, S. 1935. 3. 25, as a case in which the Conseil d'État applied a treaty which was clear. However, in that case the treaty had been implemented by a statute rather than by an executive act and the individual administrative act was held to be in violation of the statute.

[58] 1 L.N.T.S. No. 34.

ment to determine those having rights to the advantages stipulated [in the treaty] are absolutely independent of the treaty itself" and could thus be the subject of litigation in the Conseil d'État. On the merits it held for the Government. It said that by authorizing the administrative officials to deny the benefits of the treaty to those who had committed certain infractions, the Government had not intended to limit its otherwise extensive powers to police the arrangement.

The decision to take jurisdiction over the dispute was eminently reasonable, even in the context of the prevailing doctrine. Even though the entire decree was in application of a treaty, only the portion directed to the nature and quantity of the products produced in Alsace and Lorraine which were to be allowed to enter Germany duty free was in direct implementation of the treaty clause. The limitation of the benefits under the treaty to only certain exporters was a matter of domestic policy. The situation was the same as though an unrelated decree had specified that no firms which had previously engaged in fraud should be permitted to take advantage of any treaty by which French firms were to receive preferential entry to a foreign market.

The next case involving an "independent" or "detachable" administrative act two years later opened the possibility of a general control by the Conseil d'État over the implementation of treaties, a possibility which was not immediately exploited.[59] During World War I Tunisia had followed the lead of France and enacted a special war profits tax with a commission to adjudicate disputes. Because of some difficulties in the administration of appeals from the commission, a decree of the Bey of Tunis, approved by the French Resident-General, authorized the French *Commission supérieure des bénéfices de guerre* to hear the appeals. As a result of the Commission's decision that its jurisdiction was established by statute and could not be extended by a decree of the Bey of Tunis, a treaty was negotiated between France and Tunisia to authorize such appeals. The treaty was duly ratified by a decree which also specified the means by which the Commission was to implement the treaty.[60]

A complaint was brought to annul the decree in its two roles, that of the act of ratification and that of the act of implementation. The Conseil d'État had no difficulty in dismissing the first portion of the complaint. The annulment of the act of ratification would constitute the annulment of the treaty itself. This the Conseil d'État would not consider, nor will it do so now.[61]

[59] Caraco, Conseil d'État, Feb. 5, 1926, D.P. 1927. 3. 1 (note Devaux).

[60] Decree of Jan. 28, 1924, J.O. 1924. 994, D.P. 1927. 3. 3 in note. Treaty of Jan. 22, 1924, *ibid.*

[61] The Conseil d'État will refuse to apply a treaty which has not been ratified, even though it may have been published in the Official Journal, but it will not verify the legality of the decree of ratification. 1 Odent, Contentieux administratif, 1965-66 at 224-26.

To the extent the decree implemented the treaty, the Conseil d'État said it was detachable from the convention and could, therefore, be the subject of a complaint. But as before, the complainant received no satisfaction on the merits.

This decision was more than a mere affirmation of the earlier decision. The decree was a literal copy of the treaty. If this decree was independent of the treaty, it was difficult to imagine one that would not be. Moreover, the complaint went to the validity of the decree itself, not to the application of the "detachable" decree to the individual.

The new theory was a useful tool. If these two cases had been expanded to the fullest, they could have effectively eliminated all important jurisdictional restrictions on the consideration of treaties by the Conseil d'État. Not only did they give a basis for annulling individual implementing acts in conflict with "detachable" general implementing acts, but "detachable" general implementing acts could also be annulled for violation of the treaty.

They were not expanded to the fullest. There was then and continues to be at the present time, an active debate over the wisdom of the Conseil d'État intruding into any area of foreign affairs, even one which had as many "legal" elements as did treaties and even though the ordinary courts adjudicated disputes involving treaties. It was during this period of the 1920s and 1930s that the ordinary courts were engaged in their battle with the Ministry of Foreign Affairs over the impact of treaties of establishment on the rent control legislation.[62] This battle must have had an important impact on the Conseil d'État. On the one hand the courts were applying a "law" forbidden to the Conseil d'État. On the other hand the Government's reaction was a warning that it would not easily give up its prerogatives in respect to the interpretation and implementation of treaties. If the Conseil d'État was to move into this area, it would have to do so carefully.

As it turned out, progress was slow. There were no criteria to determine which implementing acts were "detachable" and which were not. Prior to World War II more often than not the implementing act was held not to be "detachable." Moreover, there were still a few kinds of treaties which the Conseil d'État considered to be Acts of Government.[63] As time went on

[62] See the discussion in Chapter III.

[63] The most striking example was Decerf, Conseil d'État, May 28, 1937, D.H. 1937. 382, S. 1937. 3. 73 (note Laroque). The Conseil d'État held that an individual had standing to contest his extradition to another country if it was pursuant to the law of March 10, 1927, D.P. 1927. 4. 265, S. 1927. L. 910, but not if it was pursuant to a treaty. The Conseil d'État first exercised jurisdiction over an extradition pursuant to a treaty in Kirkwood, Conseil d'État, May 30, 1952, S. 1953. 3. 33, 68 Rev. Dr. Pub. 781 (1952) (note Waline, concl. Letourneur). For a discussion of extradition in the criminal courts during the nineteenth century, see Chapter III.

increasing numbers of acts have been considered "detachable" and, therefore, subject to the jurisdiction of the Conseil d'État or other administrative tribunals. In 1955, for example, the Conseil d'État held for the first time that the decision of a French claims commission was detachable from the lump sum settlement agreement which it was implementing and could, therefore, be subjected to review by the administrative courts.[64]

INTERPRETATION AND THE *Acte Clair*

Although the early cases did not say so explicitly, detachable administrative acts could be annulled for being in violation of the treaty only if the treaty was an *acte clair*. Only in such a case could it be assumed that application of the treaty would not cause embarrassment to the Government in its foreign relations. The origins of the theory of the *acte clair* go back to the bifurcated nature of the French legal system.[65] It was inevitable that questions of administrative law would arise in proceedings in the courts and that questions of civil law would arise in the Conseil d'État. However, the Conseil d'État was a part of the administration rather than of the judiciary and the doctrine of the separation of powers dictated that neither the courts nor the administration, including the Conseil d'État, could decide questions of law arising out of the other legal system. In order to handle them the practice developed of suspending proceedings and referring "prejudicial questions" to the other judicial system.[66]

Naturally, the reference of a prejudicial question is time consuming, adds to the expense of litigation, and creates the possibility for delaying tactics. Therefore, the subsidiary doctrine evolved that a prejudicial question need not be referred if the text in controversy is clear, i.e. if there is an *acte clair*. In the classical explanation given by Laferrière, before it is necessary for the Conseil d'État or the courts to suspend their proceedings and pose a prejudicial question

> There must be a question: that is to say, a real difficulty raised by the parties or spontaneously recognized by the judge, and of a nature to give rise to a doubt in an intelligent intellect.[67]

[64] Deltel, Conseil d'État, Dec. 16, 1955, D. 1956. Jur. 44 (concl. Laurent).

[65] 1 Odent, Contentieux administratif, 1965-66 at 78-81; Waline, Droit administratif ¶¶ 105-08 (9e éd. 1963).

[66] The French term *question préjudicielle* has been translated literally rather than as "incidental question" or "preliminary question" so as to indicate the binding nature of the response as well as the fact that the question is posed prior to a decision on the merits.

[67] 1 Lafferière, Juridiction administrative 498.

The extent to which an act is clear will depend not only on the intelligence of the intellect, but on the judge's training and on the degree of doubt which he considers permissible. Always assuming absolute good faith, the more familiar a judge becomes with the other legal system and its philosophy, and the more he feels a part of that system, the clearer questions of law relating to it are apt to be. Over the years the training of the entire French legal profession, including those who have later become judges as well as those who have become members of the Conseil d'État, has broadened to include both civil and administrative law. Administrative law is no longer a "foreign" legal system in the courts nor is civil law so regarded in the Conseil d'État, as they all but were during the nineteenth century. Consequently, more and more acts have become clear which at an earlier time might have been thought to be unclear.[68] Even so prejudicial questions are a constant feature of the relationship between the civil courts and the Conseil d'État.

The theory of the *acte clair* was useful to the Conseil d'État in respect to treaties in that it helped overcome the political consequences of applying a treaty against the state. Since treaties were in the forbidden area of foreign affairs, the Conseil d'État could conceive of exercising authority over their implementation only if doing so would cause the Government no embarrassment. It was assumed that no embarrassment would result if the treaty was clear and the Conseil d'État was only causing the administration to fulfill the promises contracted by the Government.

The text of a treaty was clear under either of two circumstances: (1) the treaty did not need interpretation, or (2) the treaty did need interpretation but an authoritative interpretation had already been given.

This left the undesirable result that relief could not be envisioned for a private party if the text of the treaty was not clear and the Government had not yet had the occasion to interpret it. The answer to this dilemma was obvious. It was suggested by a *commissaire du gouvernement* in 1931[69] and was adopted by the Conseil d'État in *Duhamel* in 1934.[70] Suspend the proceedings and allow the parties to pose a prejudicial question to the Minister of Foreign Affairs. Once he answered, the text of the treaty would be clear and its application to the litigation at hand could cause no embarrassment to the Government.

[68] The existence of the Tribunal des Conflits, which is composed of the Minister of Justice, four high ranking members of the Conseil d'État and four from the Cour de Cassation, has also been significant. The regular contacts which this has afforded have aided in an understanding of the different points of view and of their reconciliation. 1 Odent, Contentieux administratif, 1965-66 at 447.

[69] Ettori, Conclusions in Samé, Conseil d'État, July 3, 1931, D.P. 1931. 3. 36, S. 1931. 3. 129.

[70] Conseil d'État, Oct. 26, 1934, D.H. 1935. 71, S. 1935. 3. 25 (note P. L.).

Duhamel was interesting in that it was one of the rare occasions in which an interpretation was necessary for the state to prevail.[71] Since the complainant is almost always a private individual, the refusal of the Conseil d'État to apply treaties, or treaties which were not clear, usually left the individual with no forum in which to contest the action of the state. In this case, however, the state was the moving party since it involved one of the few forms of quasi-criminal prosecution to come before the Conseil d'État.

The defendant had been acquitted by the Prefectural Council of having erected a construction within five meters of a road which formed the Franco-Belgian frontier. This limit had been agreed upon by a double declaration of the French and Belgian governments of January 15 and March 31, 1886, modifying article 69 of the Treaty of Courtrai of March 28, 1820.[72] Article 2 of the law of April 5, 1887,[73] the law which authorized the ratification of the treaty modifications, provided that any infraction of the treaty should be prosecuted as would a matter of *grande voirie*, the quasi-criminal action in the Conseil d'État for damage to certain public property.[74]

Although the penal portion of the action had lapsed because of the passage of the statute of limitations, the Conseil d'État was called upon to decide whether the structure had to be removed. The difficulty was that there was a drainage ditch on the French side of the road but not on the Belgian side. If the road included only the traveled portion, as alleged by the defendant, the structure was outside the five meter limitation. If it included the drainage ditch, as alleged by the Minister of Public Works, the construction was within five meters of the road and would have to be removed. Absent a binding interpretation, which could come only from the Minister of Foreign Affairs, the action would have had to be dismissed.

For some commentators *Duhamel* was not a great step forward but was only another indication that the Conseil d'État would not interpret treaties.[75] Perhaps they were right. Once the Conseil d'État had suspended its proceedings to allow a prejudicial question to be posed to the Minister of Foreign Affairs, it became the accepted practice. That practice continues to this day, even though the jurisdiction of the Conseil d'État over treaties is no longer based on the detachable administrative act and the *acte clair*.

Its jurisdiction is now based on article 55 of the 1958 Constitution which

[71] There had been at least one prior example. Bacri v. Le Brave, note 14 *supra*.

[72] Promulgated by decree of April 9, 1887, J.O. April 13, 1887, D.P. 1887. 4. 71.

[73] J.O. April 7, 1887, D.P. 1887. 4. 71.

[74] Waline, *Les contraventions de grande voirie ont-elles le caractère d'une infraction pénale?*, 84 Rev. Dr. Pub. 175 (1968).

[75] Rousseau, Comment, 43 Rev. Gén. Dr. Int'l. Pub. 487 (1936).

repeats the provision first found in articles 26 and 28 of the 1946 Constitution that treaties which have been properly ratified have the force of law. As a result of the constitutional provision, there is no longer the same necessity to find a detachable administrative act implementing a treaty which is or has become an *acte clair*. Such matters as extradition based on a treaty can now be handled as a problem of law rather than as one of executive privilege.[76]

With the demise of the detachable administrative act as a basis for jurisdiction, the reverse side of the theory dominates. The Conseil d'État will not accept jurisdiction over the rare nondetachable administrative acts which implement treaties. The four examples given by Odent of cases involving nondetachable administrative acts, acts "which are the necessary consequences of [the existence of] a treaty,"[77] are instructive of the new situation. These four cases involved (1) a request for indemnification for the loss of an electric utility concession in territory which had been under lease from China and which France had returned prior to the expiration of the lease and, therefore, prior to the expiration of the contract of concession;[78] (2) a request for indemnity from a man who lost his position as bailiff (*huissier*) in Hanoi as a result of the independence of North Vietnam and the subsequent treaty of judicial cooperation;[79] (3) a similar request from a former bailiff in Tunisia;[80] (4) a request for indemnity from the son of the assassinated Bey of Camp for France's failure to grant the beylical dynasty all the support promised in the treaty which established the protectorate.[81]

It is perhaps significant that these cases involved requests for damages rather than for annulment of an administrative act. In the first three cases the administrative acts complained of were so intimately tied to the treaties that their annulment would have been incompatible with the continued existence of the treaties themselves. The complainants could only ask for damages and they had to rely on such difficult grounds as the fault of the state in ratifying the treaties[82] or, alternatively, the use of damages as a means of spreading the burden of France's foreign policy over the entire nation, grounds which may soon be but have not as yet been accepted by the Conseil d'État.[83]

[76] Kirkwood, Conseil d'État, May 30, 1952, S. 1953. 3. 33, 68 Rev. Dr. Pub. 781 (1952) (note Waline, concl. Letourneur).

[77] 1 Odent, Contentieux administratif, 1965-66 at 232-33 (1966).

[78] Société indochinoise d'électricité, July 15, 1961, Rec. Cons. d'Ét. 1961. 519.

[79] Argence, Conseil d'État, Feb. 14, 1962, Rec. Cons. d'Ét. 1962. 107.

[80] Laurent, Conseil d'État, April 23, 1963, Rec. Cons. d'Ét. 1963, 247.

[81] Prince Sliman bey, Conseil d'État, March 16, 1962, D. 1962. Jur. 745 (note Silvera).

[82] Rejected as a grounds for liability of the state in Lévy, Conseil d'État, Oct. 4, 1968, Rec. Cons. d'Ét. 1968. 473.

[83] See Soulier, *Réflexion sur l'évolution et l'avenir de la responsabilité de la puissance publique*, 85 Rev. Dr. Pub. 1039, 1066-71 (1969).

The refusal to accept jurisdiction over the action brought by the son of the Bey of Camp was a different story since the allegation was that France failed to fulfill its obligations under the treaty. Perhaps this is an indication that one of the current functions of the concept of the nondetachable act is to justify the nonjusticiability of a treaty which has too many political overtones.

The recognition by the Conseil d'État that the constitution gives treaties the force of law has not only affected the detachable administrative act, it has changed the justification for the *acte clair* in respect to treaties. Originally the prejudicial question was posed to create an *acte clair* so as to confirm the precarious jurisdiction of the Conseil d'État over treaties. With the constitutional basis for the jurisdiction over treaties now well established it is no longer necessary, in a technical sense, to rely upon the *acte clair*. Instead, Lafferière's explanation of the conditions before a prejudicial question can validly be asked is now pertinent to the interpretation of a treaty as well as to questions of civil law.

> There must be a question: that is to say, a real difficulty raised by the parties or spontaneously recognized by the judge, and of a nature to give rise to a doubt in an intelligent intellect.[84]

Nevertheless, there is a self-consciousness in the Conseil d'État about the interpretation and application of treaties that one does not find in respect to civil law which suggests that the old concepts of the Act of Government are still very much alive. This is natural since the prejudicial question and the accompanying *acte clair* are considerably more politicized when treaties are concerned. Whether or not treaties should currently be called Acts of Government, they are a very special form of act "having the force of law." Their main feature is that they are a part of two or more national legal systems. Moreover, their ultimate interpreter, the Minister of Foreign Affairs, is not a different court within the French legal system. He is a political figure. His authority to interpret treaties is justified on political grounds and the interpretations given in his name are often a reflection of his political concerns.

One of the arguments raised in support of the Minister's continuing authority to interpret treaties is that he must be free to conclude binding bilateral agreements of interpretation with the foreign state or states concerned. In respect to the Conseil d'État this argument is advanced primarily as a matter of foreign affairs, but in the ordinary courts it also rests on a more

[84] 1 Lafferière, Juridiction administrative 498.

theoretical foundation of the treaty as a contract. Although the argument is attractive in the abstract, bilateral or "authentic" interpretations are seldom found in respect to the provisions of treaties subject to domestic litigation. When they are, it is even less often that they have been provoked by a prejudicial question. The usual stimulus for a bilateral interpretation of significance to the courts is the complaint to the Ministry of Foreign Affairs from the foreign state which has been injured by the judicial interpretation of the treaty.

The most often cited example of bilateral interpretations effective in the French courts is the series of agreements from 1929 to 1934 with Belgium, Great Britain, Greece, Panama, Spain, Switzerland and the United States to the effect that the pre-existing treaties of establishment between France and those countries conferred the same rights to their citizens as French citizens had under the French rent control legislation.[85] This legislation provided that French, but few foreign, lessees could extend their commercial and residential leases at their termination. On the other hand French landlords could retake the property for their personal or family use. When the ordinary courts finally succumbed under pressure to the interpretation of the treaties of establishment advocated by the Minister of Foreign Affairs, they did so because of the bilateral nature of the interpretation and without the benefit of a prejudicial question.

There is a temptation to use the bilateral interpretation as the means of creating a new agreement which goes beyond the terms of the old.[86] Of course, it is obligatory on the courts in respect to events which occur after its effective date if it is in a form to create binding domestic law.[87] However, if it is a new agreement, it should not govern events which transpired prior to its existence. More importantly for this discussion, to the extent that the bilateral interpretation is seen to be perverted from its announced function, the basis for continued judicial respect for unilateral or bilateral Governmental interpretations is undermined.

[85] See the discussion *in extenso* in Chapter III of the events which led to these agreements and to the consequences which followed.

[86] Raynaud, Note to Zumkeller v. Florence, Cas. civ., Feb. 4, 1936, S. 1936. I. 257; Perroud, Note to Sanchez v. Gozland, Cass. civ., Dec. 22, 1931, 59 Clunet 683, 713 (1932).

[87] During the confrontation over the lease legislation some lower courts considered the bilateral interpretations to be new agreements which required parliamentary approval prior to ratification if they were to be binding on the courts, e.g., Société Suchard v. Cauchin, Trib. civ. Seine, March 8, 1932, 59 Clunet 965 (1932). See the conclusions of the *procureur général* Matter in Sanchez v. Gozland, Cass. civ., Dec. 22, 1931, D.P. 1932. I. 131, 134, 59 Clunet 683, 687. However, at the present time both the courts and the Conseil d'État will enforce international agreements which have been ratified by the President, whether or not the required parliamentary approval was previously given for the ratification. Dehaussy, *Les traités*, Juris-Classeur, Droit International, fasc. 12-A, ¶ 76 (1959).

Considerations of foreign affairs exist even though no bilateral interpretation is expected. Normally such considerations are of significance only if the interpretation by the tribunal could be expected to be adverse to the interests of the foreign state. On rare occasions a ruling favorable to the interests of the foreign state can be adverse to France's foreign interests.[88] If these considerations of foreign affairs are such as to give the basis for a legal interpretation of the treaty in the manner advocated by the Government, there is little reason why they could not be transmitted to the Conseil d'État for its use in interpreting the treaty.

The problem becomes more acute when the Government wishes a particular interpretation of a treaty for political reasons which the Conseil d'État would find hard to accept if the treaty were just another legal norm. When such cases arise, it is undoubtedly with some degree of relief along with a degree of chagrin that the Conseil d'État finds that it cannot interpret the treaty but must refer it to the Minister of Foreign Affairs. It is often thought to be less incompatible with the judicial nature of a tribunal to receive and act upon a politically motivated judgment of another than it is for that same tribunal to render its judgment on the basis of those same political factors.

In spite of the objections to the practice, the reference of prejudicial questions to the Minister of Foreign Affairs is potentially a useful device. Except for article 177 in the Treaty of Rome and the parallel provisions in other Community treaties, it is the only means presently available to assure a uniform interpretation and application of treaties either within France[89] or between France and the other country or countries concerned.

This is of particular importance because the Minister of Foreign Affairs does not have a monopoly of the conduct of foreign affairs.[90] The various ministries deal directly with their foreign counterparts in solving the substantive problems which they have in common. In spite of a decree of March 14, 1953, which stated that "[t]he Minister of Foreign Affairs is alone charged with providing for the ratification and the publication of conventions, agreements, protocols and international settlements to which France is a signatory or by which France is bound [,]"[91] the Ministry of Foreign Affairs has been unable to achieve even this formal monopoly in respect to treaties.[92] The decree itself excepted international labor conventions, the ratification

[88] One such occasion was Trouttman, Cass. req., July 24, 1861, D.P. 1861. 1. 342 (concl. Dupin), S. 1861. 1. 687, discussed in Chapter III.

[89] See *Publication des engagements internationaux*, [1962] Ann. Fr. Dr. Int'l. 888, 895.

[90] *Ibid.* at 897.

[91] Decree No. 53-192 of March 14, 1953, J.O. 1953. 2436, D. 1953. L. 94.

[92] See *Publication des engagements internationaux*, [1962] Ann. Fr. Dr. Int'l. at 897; Rousseau *Le régime actuel de publication des traités en France*, D. 1953. chron. 169.

and promulgation of which were to be provided for jointly with the Minister of Labor. In practice there is a great disorder and many international agreements come into effect without the participation of the Ministry of Foreign Affairs.

The situation is even more chaotic in respect to the administrative interpretation and application of treaties where the authority is spread throughout the administration. There appears to be no formal mechanism to assure uniformity other than the practice of the Conseil d'État and of the courts to refer prejudicial questions to the Minister of Foreign Affairs when they arise in litigation.

However, neither bilateral interpretation, considerations of foreign policy, nor uniformity is sufficient to justify Governmental interpretation unless the interpretations given are of a consistently high quality. There is little published on who within the Ministry of Foreign Affairs determines the appropriate interpretation of a treaty, the meaning of which either the Conseil d'État or the courts has already determined not to be clear. Since the Minister himself will be involved only in rare cases, the interpretation will usually be given by second rank personnel on the recommendation of lower level personnel. Similarly, there has been little discussion of the manner in which the interpretation is decided. Presumably, the Ministry searches its files on the negotiations leading to the drafting of the provision in question. Officially the Ministry does not hear counsel and if representations are made to it privately, no record appears. The resulting picture is that of anonymous bureaucrats deciding the ultimate question in a lawsuit without the benefit of public debate by counsel or the other procedural regularities which are normally available for the decision before the Conseil d'État or the courts.

Even worse is the picture painted by Professor Chrétien in his study of the interpretation of tax treaties. Since the Ministry of Foreign Affairs has little, if any, expertise in the matter, it is understandable that it would turn for help to the technically competent Ministry of Finance, the ministry which in fact negotiates tax treaties. It appears that on all but rare occasions the interpretation is determined there.[93] However, the tax collector with whom the individual is litigating is also in the Ministry of Finance. It is little wonder that the interpretation given by the Minister of Foreign Affairs is loaded in favor of the tax authorities.[94] In fact, no matter what the subject of litigation,

[93] Chrétien, *L'application et l'interprétation des clauses fiscales des traités internationaux par les tribunaux français*, 40 Rev. Cr. D.I.P. 41, 61 (1951).

[94] *Ibid.* Professor Chrétien reported in 1951 that he could find one instance in which the Minister of Foreign Affairs interpreted a tax treaty in a manner favorable to the taxpayer.

when the Conseil d'État requests the Minister of Foreign Affairs to interpret a treaty, the interpretation given systematically supports the position previously taken by the administration.[95]

On balance it would seem that the Conseil d'État should make some move towards establishing its authority to interpret treaties. Every year it receives a number of cases in which the implications for France's foreign affairs are not significant. These cases typically involve the domestic administration of commitments made by treaty, problems about which the Conseil d'État knows considerably more than does the Minister of Foreign Affairs.[96] The Conseil d'État could, perhaps, adopt the formula currently in use by several of the civil chambers of the Cour de Cassation, namely, that it has the authority to interpret a treaty unless the interpretation would raise questions of public international law.

Why doesn't it do so? One reason is undoubtedly the felt need to proceed slowly into an area of perceived delicacy. The Conseil d'État's current jurisdiction over treaties was not acquired until long after the confirmation of its authority over other law creating acts. The doctrine of the detachable administrative act dates from 1924, the reference of the prejudicial question so that the treaty could become an *acte clair* dates from 1934 and the recognition of the treaty as having the "force of law" under the constitution dates only from 1952.

A second reason may be based on yet another aspect of the *acte clair*. The Conseil d'État can determine not only whether there is a "question" as defined by Laferrière, but whether it is politically wiser to refer a prejudicial question than to decide the matter itself. A determination that a treaty provision is clear to the Conseil d'État, although it is obscure to most people, sets little precedent. In the next case, if necessary, a provision which is clear to most may be obscure to the Conseil d'État. With the secrecy of the deliberations closely guarded and opinions which are less than explanatory, there is no way to know the extent to which the decision to refer or not to refer a prejudicial question was based on the perceived clarity of the text and to what extent it was based on political considerations. It may even be that the members of the Conseil d'État do not know for sure the basis on which their colleagues voted one way or the other. Such a flexible and noninformative doctrine may give the Conseil d'État more freedom to interpret treaties

[95] Dubouis, *Le juge administratif français et les règles du droit international*, [1971] Ann. Fr. Dr. Int'l. 9, 40.

[96] Silz, note to Société Alkan & Cie, Conseil d'État, June 11, 1937, D.P. 1939. 3. 47 at 52.

in fact than it would have under a more explicit and permissive doctrine.[97]

Although all courts find it necessary at times to trim their sails in the face of political pressure, the Conseil d'État is in an unusually delicate position. It handles litigation of great significance to the Government and yet it has developed an enviable reputation for its independence. It has been able to achieve this independence only by a constant awareness of the weakness of its institutional setting and by adjusting to this weakness.

One aspect of this institutional weakness is that members of the Conseil d'État are not protected by the rule applicable to the ordinary courts that judges may not be removed from office except for misfeasance.[98] The Conseil d'État is an advisary body within the administration and its members are subject to dismissal with very few formal protections. For a long time this had been forgotten.

From 1872 when the Conseil d'État was delegated the authority to decide cases in its own name a *de facto* immunity from dismissal had developed.[99] Even under the Vichy regime a member of the Conseil d'État who had spoken out publicly against Marshall Petain and in favor of General de Gaulle had only been relieved from his administrative assignment, not from the corps. This had led to some euphoria in respect to the independence of the Conseil d'État.

Then in 1960 a young member of the Conseil d'État was dismissed from the corps for disagreeing with de Gaulle's policies in Algeria. While he had been assigned to administrative duties rather than to judicial duties on the Section du contentieux, his dismissal was seen as raising serious doubts of the inviolability of office of those exercising the judicial function.[100]

What was a serious doubt in 1960 became a serious fear in 1962 following

[97] "When a text is clear and simple, it needs only to be applied. If, starting from this point of view, one were to decide that there is a necessity to refer to the Minister of Foreign Affairs for interpretation only in the case of ambiguity or real obscurity, one would considerably reduce the number of references, especially if the Conseil d'État, sovereign judge of whether there is obscurity or ambiguity, showed itself little disposed to find one or the other.... For international treaties... one could legitimately think that a very real obscurity or ambiguity must be required before recognizing the existence of a difficulty requiring interpretation." *Ibid.*

[98] The rule in respect to judges of the ordinary courts is found in article 64 of the Constitution, and in ordonnance No. 58-1270, art. 4, of Dec. 22, 1958, J.O. 1958. 11551, D. 1959. L. 21. Although this rule has been too often violated in the purges which have followed most major changes in regime, these violations have been recognized as extraordinary events and the rule continues to give the judges of the ordinary courts a degree of personal independence. 1 Solus and Perrot, Droit judiciare privé ¶ 782 (1961).

[99] Drago, *Some Recent Reforms of the French Conseil d'État*, 13 Int. Comp. L. Q. 1282, 1288 (1964).

[100] Morange, *Les principes généraux du droit sous la Ve Républic*, 76 Rev. Dr. Pub. 1188 (1960).

the decision of the Conseil d'État in the *Canal* case.[101] In *Canal* the Conseil d'État annulled the ordonnance by which General de Gaulle had created a special military court to deal with the Secret Army Organization, a terrorist organization pledged to prevent de Gaulle from conceding Algeria's independence.

The Government's reaction was immediate and threatened a direct confrontation. Five days after the decision was rendered the Council of Ministers issued an official statement which said in part that the Conseil d'État had "exceeded its jurisdiction as a court of law." M. Fouchet, the Minister of Information, stated that "[t]he Government acknowledges the existence of the *Canal* judgment, but takes the view that it is of no effect."[102]

Although the Government's reaction became less extreme with time, one result was the creation of a working group to examine possible changes in the organization and working of the Conseil d'État. The creation of this working group less than three months following the *Canal* decision led to the fear that there would be restrictions on the traditional competence of the Conseil d'État.

> Some expected that, at a minimum, the Conseil d'État would no longer be competent in respect to the regulatory power exercised in the legislative domain by means of ordonnances.
>
> A few even went so far as to suggest that every decision deliberated by the Council of Ministers would escape the censure of the (Conseil d'État).
>
> There would thus have been an enlargment of the notion of the Act of Government, at a time when the concurrent tendency of the doctrine and the case law is going in the direction of restricting it.[103]

The report of the working group did not go this far. But its proposals would have significantly increased the Government's control over both the internal operations of the Conseil d'État and its senior personnel. The most spectacular proposal was to lower the retirement age from 70 to 60 allowing those who wished to continue their service to apply to the Government for reappointment at ages 60 and 65.[104] The increased ease with which the Government could rid itself of inconvenient individuals was all too evident.

The strong reaction to these proposals may well have been the factor which persuaded the Government not to carry out the more objectionable

[101] Canal, Conseil d'État, Oct. 19, 1962, D. 1962. Jur. 687, S. 1963. Jur. 32.

[102] Quoted in Drago, *Some Recent Reforms* 1283.

[103] Silvera, *La réforme du Conseil d'État*, S. 1963. chron. 51, 59.

[104] Drago, *Some Recent Reforms* 1284. The working group recommended that the application be referred to an advisory commission whose advice the Government would be bound to follow.

among them. "The important thing [was] that the Conseil d'État [was] not changed out of all recognition, and that it [could] continue with its work."[105] Nevertheless, the Conseil d'État had received an object lesson. It is vulnerable to "reform" at the instigation of a provoked Government.

There is still considerable merit in being careful in the extension of jurisdiction into matters which have traditionally been free of judicial scrutiny and in which the Government continues to evidence an interest. While it may be time to venture into the explicit interpretation of some treaties, the doctrine of the *acte clair* remains a convenient screen behind which the Conseil d'État can build a practice of limited interpretation until the day when it feels free to do more.

SUPREMACY

The assertion by the monists of the supremacy of treaty over statute, the consecration of this principle in the 1946 and 1958 Constitutions,[106] and the ratification of the Community treaties have led many to call for the Conseil d'État to assure the supremacy of treaty over statute.

It is hardly suprising that the Conseil d'État has not responded to this call with enthusiasm. The enforcement by the national courts of a general doctrine of the supremacy of treaties is not viable in the current world. There are both technical and political difficulties to the drafting of those treaties intended to create positive law within the state which are not generally experienced in domestic law making. These difficulties include such matters as divergent legal systems into which the new treaty must fit; different languages, with the effect this has on the precision of translations and on the use of words of art; the greater diversity of interests which must be considered; and the fact that the negotiation and ratification of treaties involves more persons and institutions than does the enactment of a statute. The result is too often a text which can be inserted into the domestic legal system only with difficulty.[107]

As difficult as it is to draft such treaties, it is often more difficult to amend them. "In comparing the treaty process to domestic law making, we are

[105] *Ibid.* 1299.

[106] "Treaties or agreements duly ratified or approved shall, upon their publication, have an authority superior to that of laws, subject, for each agreement or treaty, to its application by the other party." Article 55 of the Constitution of October 4, 1958, J.O. 1958. 9151, D. 1958. L. 324 (English translation, French Embassy, Press and Information Service).

[107] For the reactions of one participant to an international conference for the drafting of a treaty unifying the international law of sales, see Honnold, *The Uniform Law for the International Sale of Goods: The Hague Convention of 1964*, 30 Law & Cont. Prob. 326, 328-32, 349-53 (1965).

struck by the fact that a law, or even a constitutional provision, is subject to the possibility of more liberal amendment than a treaty."[108] Without an adequate amendment process, treaties soon become out of date. This is especially true for those treaties which deal with technical economic problems.[109] The Government may find that it must denounce an entire treaty in order to free itself from a provision which it can no longer accept. As an alternative the legislature must be free to meet the needs of society as they arise without being precluded from doing so by a treaty.

Even if a generalized supremacy of treaty over statute were desirable, it would be unrealistic to expect the Conseil d'État to assure that supremacy before it is willing to assert authority over the interpretation of treaties. Moreover, it would be irrelevant for most purposes whether the treaty was superior to the statute so long as treaties are routinely sent to the Minister of Foreign Affairs for interpretation. It is the rare treaty which does not raise at least the implicit question whether it was intended to preclude later national legislation of the type in question.

On more than one occasion, the Minister of Foreign Affairs has consciously used his authority to interpret treaties as the means of ensuring that a given treaty or the conflicting statute would be applied.[110] The formal supremacy of treaty or statute has not been the controlling issue. Therefore, the assertion in the Conseil d'État of the formal supremacy of treaty over statute is an issue in only two cases. The first case involves an earlier treaty which clearly was meant to preclude the subsequent legislation so that no prejudicial question is necessary. The second case arises when the Minister of Foreign Affairs is precluded from interpreting the treaty. As a practical matter, the second possibility is restricted to the various Community treaties.

The problem of formal treaty supremacy is especially difficult for the Conseil d'État because the primary argument for the supremacy of treaties over statutes relies upon article 55 of the 1958 Constitution which declares that treaties "have an authority superior to laws." The assertion by a tribunal of the supremacy of a treaty over a statute would necessarily require that tribunal to declare the statute in violation of article 55. However, the Conseil d'État has never claimed the authority to determine the constitutionality of statutes and it does not appear to be ready to begin now some one hundred

[108] Kaplan and Katzenbach, The Political Foundations of International law 244 (1961).

[109] See Durand, *Transports internationaux: où en sont les Conventions de Berne?*, J.C.P. 1972. I. 2444.

[110] There is no better example than the history of the controversy over the lease legislation and the *carte de commerçant* described in Chapter III.

eighty years after the revolutionaries first restricted the courts to the application of the laws.[111]

Nor should the Conseil d'État attempt to control the constitutionality of statutes. Its role is to control the executive and it needs all of its limited assets in this task. All courts are inherently weak in comparison to the political organs of the state. If they achieve any semblance of authority in their relationship with those institutions, it is only because they have allied themselves with some other power.

The authority of the Conseil d'État over the acts of the administration and to a lesser but nevertheless significant extent over those of the Government has been achieved in large part through its constant insistence on the necessity to adhere to the statutory norms. The Conseil d'État has done more than recognize the supremacy of Parliament, it has insisted upon the supremacy of Parliament. This has not only brought the Parliament to its aid in specific disputes with the Government, it has given the Conseil d'État a set of norms outside the executive to which it could turn to control the executive. The various constitutions would not have served as well. The Parliament has continued in one form or another, the constitutions have gone with the regimes they represented.

The cost to the Conseil d'État, if indeed this is a cost, is that it dare not undercut its ally by diminishing any further the supremacy of Parliament.

The reduced role of the Parliament under the Fifth Republic is necessarily bringing changes to the Conseil d'État. On the one hand the Parliament is a less significant ally than it was in the past. On the other hand there is less reason to be concerned with its actions. The Parliament usually enacts only the "fundamental principles" while the details are supplied by regulation.[112] Conflicts are more apt to arise over the details of application than over the fundamental principles. It will be enough if the Conseil d'État is able to continue its effective control over these details.

[111] Among the many authors who stress the difficulty for a French court, and especially the Conseil d'État, to control the constitutionality of a statute in conflit with a treaty, Batailler, Le Conseil d'État: Juge constitutionnel 278-83 (1966); 1 Odent, Contentieux administratif, 1965-66 at 229-32.

[112] Article 34 of the Constitution of October 4, 1958, J.O. 1958. 9151, D. 1958. L. 324.

CHAPTER III

TREATIES IN THE COURTS

The law in respect to the interpretation and application of treaties has developed in an entirely different way in the ordinary courts than it did in the Conseil d'État, even though the law has been affected in both judicial systems by the same concern not to interfere with the conduct of France's foreign relations. That concern was expressed in the Conseil d'État in the formula that a treaty was an Act of Government. Among other things, this formula implied that treaties were negotiated, ratified, and applied by the Government rather than by the administration. Since the Conseil d'État is a part of the administration rather than the Government, it had no jurisdiction over such acts.

The parallel and fundamental problem in the courts has been that treaties are acts of the executive. Since the doctrine of the separation of powers leaves the courts limited authority over executive acts, it has been natural to ask the question of the court's authority over treaties. In order to understand the context in which this question has been answered, it will be useful to note some of the peculiarities of French court organization and procedure which implement the doctrine of the separation of powers.

PROCEDURES TO CONTROL A SUSPECT INSTITUTION

The revolutionaries of 1789 did not trust the courts to apply the law in the new spirit of the times.[1] As a result the courts were prohibited from issuing regulations, as had been their habit during the *ancien régime*, from interfering in any manner with the operations of the administration, or from inquiring into the validity of legislation once it was published.

[1] The following history is taken from Gény, Method of Interpretation and Sources of Private Positive Law ¶¶ 41-45 (2nd ed. 1954).

The courts were also expected to interpret the law to the minimum necessary. To that end they were invited to refer to the legislature any questions of interpretation which might come before them.[2] At a later time a system of mandatory referral for the interpretation of legislation was attempted before the entire system was abandoned. But it was abandoned only because it did not work in practice, not because it was considered to be bad theory.

In order to be sure that the courts were fulfilling their obligations in the proper manner, a new institution unknown to the *ancien régime* was created, the Tribunal de Cassation later renamed the Cour de Cassation. It was created as an adjunct to the legislature rather than as a supreme court.

In formal theory even today the Cour de Cassation is not regarded as a court.[3] A court has jurisdiction over a case, which means in French theory that it is the judge of law and fact in the dispute and can render a final judgment. The Cour de Cassation, however, is not a judge of the facts and cannot render a judgment in the case. It is authorized only to consider the questions of law presented to it. If the Cour de Cassation finds no impropriety in the decision of the court of appeal, it rejects the petition for *cassation.* If it finds a misinterpretation or misapplication of the law, it quashes the judgment and sends the case to a new court of appeal for further proceedings.[4]

Of the several prohibitions placed on the courts the one which has most affected the subsequent developments – and especially those in respect to treaties – was the prohibition against interfering with the administration.[5] Interference could occur in many different ways, e.g. an official might be called to answer for some act carried out in the performance of his duties, damages or other relief might be claimed against the state, or the validity of an administrative act might be challenged in the course of private litigation.

A number of procedural devices have been created to police the prohibition of interfering with the administration. The most obvious is that on the appeal of the losing party the Cour de Cassation can quash the decision below on the grounds that the court exceeded its powers (*excès de pouvoir*) and violated the doctrine of the separation of powers.

[2] Cuche et Vincent, Précis de procédure civile et commerciale ¶ 127 (12e éd. 1960).

[3] *Ibid.*; 1 Solus et Perrot, Droit judiciare privé ¶ 678 (1961).

[4] The verb *casser* means to break. The Cour de Cassation breaks or quashes the decision below; it does not reverse the decision as does an American appellate court.

For a variety of theoretical reasons going to the history of the creation of the Cour de Cassation and to the role it was expected to play, the court to which the case is returned is not required to follow the opinion of the Cour de Cassation. Therefore, it is necessary to return the case to a new court of appeal which has not already considered the matter. See Gény, Method of Interpretation at 45.

[5] Decree of Aug. 16-24, 1790, Title II, art. 13, S. 1789-1830. L. 49.

If the court acted in excess of its power by accepting jurisdiction over a case which the courts are not to hear, the decision below is simply quashed and no further judicial proceedings take place. However, if the court properly had jurisdiction over the dispute but exceeded its powers in the resolution of that dispute, the Cour de Cassation will quash the decision and send the case to a new court of appeal for further proceedings.

This latter procedure has been frequently used to quash decisions which interpreted administrative acts. The courts are to apply an administrative act only if it is clear. If it is not clear, they have to stay their proceedings in order to receive an interpretation from the appropriate administrative authority which will render the meaning clear for the benefit of the court.[6] During the nineteenth century the courts began to interpret administrative acts of a regulatory character and their competence to do so was affirmed in 1923 by the Tribunal des Conflits.[7] The restriction on the authority of the courts to interpret administrative acts is presently limited to individual acts of a non-regulatory character and, under some circumstances, to treaties.

Since the question whether the court had improperly interpreted an administrative act is one which goes to the allocation of the power of the state and is, therefore, a question of public policy, until 1958 it could be raised by the parties at any stage of the proceedings, even before the Cour de Cassation.[8] It could even be raised by the Cour de Cassation on its own motion.[9]

Now that it is clear that the courts will neither attempt to undo the work of the Revolution of 1789 nor attempt to interfere with the administration as they did during the *ancien régime*, the need for an orderly procedure has taken precedence and all defenses of lack of jurisdiction must be raised prior to defenses on the merits.[10]

While it could be expected that the defendant would himself normally raise any possible objection to the jurisdiction of the court, the matter was considered of such urgency that the Government was given two extraordinary procedures by which it can intervene in private litigation if a court is violating the separation of powers. One of them is commenced by the prefect of the department in which the litigation is in progress by the filing of a *déclinatoire*

[6] Since the late nineteenth century the appropriate administrative authority has normally been the Conseil d'État. 4 Odent, Contentieux administratif 1965-66, pp. 1373-75.

[7] Septfonds, Tribunal des Conflits, June 16, 1923, D.P. 1924. 3. 41 (concl. Matter), S. 1923. 3. 49 (note Hauriou).

[8] Cuche et Vincent, Procédure civile et commerciale ¶ 271 bis.

[9] Yter, Cass. crim., July 27, 1877, D.P. 1878. 1. 137 (rapport Gast, note Béquet), S. 1877. 1. 485.

[10] C. Pro. Civ., art. 168, as amended by decree No. 58-1289 of Dec. 22, 1958, art. 3, J.O. 1958, 11608, D. 1959. L. 45.

de conflit with the court.[11] The prefect alleges in the *déclinatoire* that the court is exceeding its authority either because the litigation is within the competence of the administrative authorities or because the court is about to interpret an administrative act which can be interpreted only by the administrative authorities. In the *déclinatoire* the prefect invites the court to dismiss the case. If the court does so, the plaintiff can appeal to the court of appeal. If either the trial court or the court of appeal rules that the courts have jurisdiction, the prefect can "raise" the conflict before the Tribunal des Conflits which makes a final and binding decision.

The second of the extraordinary remedies is the petition for *excès de pouvoir*.[12] It can be brought only by the Procureur Général before the Cour de Cassation on the direction of the Minister of Justice. It can be brought against any ruling of any court, not only a final judgment. Since its purpose is political in protection of the separation of powers and is not in aid of resolving the dispute, it can be brought at any time, even before the losing party has had the opportunity to appeal the adverse ruling. It is brought directly before the Cour de Cassation, bypassing any court of appeal which would normally be competent. If any *excès de pouvoir* is found, the Cour de Cassation annuls the offending act with binding effect on all parties.

The distinction between the ordinary petition for *cassation* by the losing party on the grounds of an *excès de pouvoir* and the petition for *excès de pouvoir* by the Procureur Général must be kept in mind. One is no more than the standard petition of a losing party looking for grounds on which the decision below might be reversed. The other is a device to protect society, and the impact on the parties to the dispute is of secondary importance. Both of course protect the administration from the interference of the courts.

THE CLASSICAL PERIOD 1789 TO 1914

Interpretation

Treaties did not present a major problem to the pre-Revolutionary courts. They were considered to be contracts between sovereigns in regard to their affairs, one might almost say their personal affairs. They were concerned with marriage settlements, peace and alliance for war. Provisions likely to affect

[11] The procedure of *conflit* is described in all texts on administrative law. E.g., 1 de Laubadère, Droit administratif ¶¶ 652-78; 1 Odent, Contentieux administratif 1965-66, pp. 431-72; Waline, Droit administratif ¶¶ 66-87.

[12] The petition for *excès de pouvoir* is presently governed by law No. 47-1366 of July 23, 1947, art. 52, J.O. 1947. 7142, D. 1947. L. 275.

private litigation were rare, except to the extent that a cession of territory affected the court and sometimes the substantive law applicable, and were usually an incidental feature of a broader concern.[13] There was no doubt that an applicable treaty would be enforced in the courts. The King was the sole source of law. His treaties were as binding upon his subjects and officials as were his decrees.[14]

With the Revolution the formal unity of legislative and treaty making powers was split. Laws were enacted by the legislature. Treaties were promulgated by the King, and later by the Emperor or other head of state. The various constitutions since 1791 have contained many variants on the distribution of the legislative power but the treaty making power was always an executive prerogative and legislative ratification of treaties was rarely required until 1875. Since treaties were no longer adopted in the same manner and by the same person as statutes and other domestic law, it was no longer self-evident that they should be treated in the same manner by the courts.

Nevertheless, with few exceptions, during the early years following the Revolution the judicial courts continued to apply treaties as domestic law as they had during the *ancien régime*. The classic expression of this stage of French thinking was given by Merlin in his conclusions as Procureur Général to the Cour de Cassation in a case decided in 1811.

> The treaty of January 11, 1787, was a law for France as it was for Russia. It was published in France immediately after its signature. No French court can ignore it.[15]

In 1811 there was little more reason to differentiate between a domestic law and a treaty than there had been during the *ancien régime*. The Emperor was all-powerful in fact, even if not completely in legal theory. Although a legislature continued to exist, the dividing line between law and regulation was blurred because the ultimate decision as to the use either of laws and Senatus-consults or of regulations, decrees and orders had been placed in his hands.

By 1839, when the modern law of treaties began in a case decided by the Cour de Cassation, it was no longer possible to accept without question Merlin's statement that a treaty "was a law for France." King Louis-Phillippe

[13] The major exceptions were the treaties restricting or abolishing the *droit d'aubaine*. The list of the treaties existing as of 1801 is in 2 Locré, La législation de la France 118-22 (1827). The *droit d'aubaine* prevented aliens from taking by will or intestate succession property held in a state by either aliens or citizens.

[14] Clunet, *Du défaut de validité de plusieurs traités diplomatiques conclus par la France avec les puissances étrangères*, 7 Clunet 5, 6 (1880).

[15] Merlin's conclusions are reported in 16 Merlin, Répertoire universel et raissoné de jurisprudence 194, 205 (5e éd. 1828). The case itself is Champeaux-Grammont v. Cardon, Cass. civ., July 15, 1811, S. 1809-11. 1. 377.

was not all-powerful. The Charter of 1814, which had established a constitutional monarchy, had been amended in 1830 to reduce further the royal prerogative before Louis-Phillippe had been offered the throne. As before, laws could be adopted only with the consent of the Chamber of Peers, the Chamber of Deputies and the King, but henceforth the King could not suspend their operation by a royal ordonnance. This was in response to the attempted *coup d'état* by Charles X who had dissolved the Chamber of Deputies twice in two months, had reintroduced censorship of the press and had changed the electoral laws by royal ordonnance.[16]

In spite of the great concern over the King's power to legislate, the Charter gave the two Chambers no role in respect to treaties. Treaties remained the King's prerogative alone.[17]

The split between the legislative law making process and the executive treaty making process raised difficult questions for the courts. On the one hand was the question whether a treaty, even though it did not receive legislative approval, could still be considered a "law" with all that implied in respect to such matters as the courts' authority to enforce it, to interpret it, and to reconcile it with a conflicting statute. On the other hand was the question whether the courts had any authority in respect to the treaty if treaties were executive acts. If they did, it would still be necessary to establish the status of the treaty in respect to conflicting statutes.

Some kind of an answer to these questions had already been given by the Conseil d'État. It would not accept jurisdiction of a dispute if the complaint was either based on or in conflict with a treaty. While the most important of these decisions had been in cases of great political sensitivity, by 1839 it seemed to be a general rule. Treaties were already referred to in the literature about administrative law as Acts of Government, a designation which not only implied much the same thing as "political question" in the United States, but which indicated that the treaty was seen by the Conseil d'État as an act of executive policy rather than an act creating law.

The 1839 case in which the Cour de Cassation first faced these questions involved the ownership of Aubigny, a former feudal domain.[18] It had been owned by the Third Duke of Richmond, an English subject, when it was sequestered in 1806, during the middle of the Napoleonic Wars. Less than two months latter the Duke died leaving as his heirs four sisters and several

[16] The amendments to the Charter in 1830 in respect to the royal legislative authority are discussed by Sieghart, Government by Decree 173-75 (1950).

[17] Charter of 1830, art. 13, 18 D. Rép. 333, S. 1789-1830. L. 1234.

[18] Napier v. Lennox, Duke of Richmond, Cass. civ., June 24, 1839, S. 1839. 1. 577, Jour. Pal. 1839. 2. 208 (concl. Dupin).

nephews, the sons of a deceased brother. The oldest nephew became the Fourth Duke of Richmond. It was in these circumstances that a secret annex to article 4 of the treaty of peace of May 30, 1814, stipulated that the sequestration of Aubigny was lifted and "the Duke of Richmond" should recover his property. A royal ordonnance implementing the treaty provision was issued the following July 8, followed by an order of the prefect of the Department of the Cher on August 3, 1814, putting the Fourth Duke of Richmond in possession.

Sometime later the four sisters of the Third Duke brought suit in the French courts for a division of the property according to the French law of succession. They each claimed a one-fifth share with the remaining fifth going to the Fifth Duke, who had succeeded to Aubigny on the death of his father. The defendant claimed that the secret article which lifted the sequestration and returned the property to "the Duke of Richmond" specifically referred to the Duke of Richmond then alive in 1814, i.e. his father, the Fourth Duke. His great-aunts claimed that it referred to the Third Duke from whom the property had been sequestered and that on the death of the Third Duke in 1806 his claim to the return of Aubigny had passed to his heirs.

The trial court could see no reason from the wording of the clause in the treaty why this property should not be subject to the normal rules of intestate succession and upheld the claim of the plaintiffs.[19] However, the Court of Appeal of Bourges held that the courts had no authority to search for the meaning of a clause in a treaty, royal ordonnance and prefectoral order which purely and simply restored the possession of Aubigny to the Duke of Richmond. For the plaintiffs to prevail they "must, if it is possible, raise the question of the effect of the acts mentioned above before the competent authority. Until then these acts remain in all their force and are an obstacle to [the plaintiffs'] action." As a result the court of appeal dismissed the case for lack of jurisdiction.

The court of appeal had based its decision on the prohibition against the judicial courts from interfering with the administrative authorities. It did not indicate whether its action was based on the fact that the treaty had been specifically implemented by the executive when Aubigny was restored to the Fourth Duke of Richmond, thereby implicitly interpreting the treaty in his favor, or whether it believed that all treaties were of such a nature that they

[19] The decisions of the trial court and of the Court of Appeal of Bourges are printed with the report of the Cour de Cassation in the Journal du Palais.

could not be interpreted by the courts.[20] Nor did the court indicate to which administrative authority the plaintiffs should go in order to receive an interpretation which would be acceptable to it. That was always for the parties to determine after the court had indicated that an administrative interpretation was necessary. The Procureur Général before the Cour de Cassation wondered whether the plaintiffs were to be required to petition a new congress of the sovereigns who had negotiated the treaty to interpret it for the purpose of this dispute.[21]

The Civil Chamber of the Cour de Cassation quashed the decision of the court of appeal. It noted that once a court has jurisdiction of a complaint, it has jurisdiction over any defenses raised to the complaint unless there is a law prescribing otherwise. The defendant had improperly invoked the principle that the civil courts cannot interpret administrative acts. The Civil Chamber explained that

> Treaties adopted between nations are not simple acts of administration and execution. They have the character of law and can be applied and interpreted only in the manner and by the authorities charged to apply all the laws in the area of their competence every time that the context which gives rise to this interpretation has for its object private interests.[22]

The decision was significant in three respects. First, it affirmed that the courts could apply treaties which come before them. After this decision there was never to be any serious challenge to their self-executing nature in the courts even though the Conseil d'État would not enforce them for almost another hundred years. Secondly, the decision affirmed that the courts could interpret at least some treaties. Thirdly, it introduced language which suggested that the competence of the courts to interpret treaties was limited to those matters involving private interests. This point will be discussed at length below.

A fourth matter which appeared to be settled was the suggestion that treaties were administrative acts which could be interpreted only by the administrative authorities. However, this characterization of treaties was hard to extinguish so long as they were negotiated and ratified by the executive without legislative approval. In two cases decided in 1851 and 1852 the

[20] It was still unsettled in 1839 whether the courts had the authority to interpret generally administrative acts of a regulatory character. Matter, conclusions in Septfonds, Tribunal des Conflits, June 16, 1923, D.P. 1924. 3. 41.

[21] Jour. Pal. 1839. 2. 208, 213.

[22] S. 1839. 1. 577, 579, Jour. Pal. 1839. 2. 208, 218.

Criminal Chamber of the Cour de Cassation referred to treaties of extradition as measures "of high administration" which only the contracting powers could interpret.[23]

However, these cases were not good examples either of treaties as administrative acts or for the deference of the courts to the interpretation of treaties by the executive. The deference of the courts to the executive in extradition cases was not a result of the law of treaties. Until the enactment of the law of March 10, 1927 the courts could question neither the validity of the events which had led to a defendant's presence in France nor the procedure by which a foreigner was placed in custody for the purpose of banishment.[24] The natural law publicists in the seventeenth and eighteenth centuries had developed the theory that the right both to request the extradition of an alleged criminal who had fled the country and the right to render over the alleged criminal to the foreign sovereign was a personal right of the sovereign himself.[25] As late as 1827 the Cour de Cassation stated that extradition was based on the royal birthright, not on any treaty or other agreement between the two countries.[26]

Until the law of 1927 established a procedure for the extradition of alleged criminals to and from France, extradition was completely political in its motivations and administrative in its operation. Certain practices had developed between the states governing extradition, such as the rule that there would be no extradition for a political offense. These rules were enforced by the Minister of Justice on his subordinates to assure the continuation of good relations with the extraditing state.[27] The attitude of the courts was that the commencement of the prosecution was a determination by the Government that the extradition had been proper. On the rare occasions when the peculiarities of the case raised the possibility that the Minister of Justice might wish to overrule his subordinates, the courts stayed their proceedings awaiting his decision.[28]

All of this was true whether or not there was a treaty. While the Criminal Chamber had been correct in saying that only the two Governments could

[23] Viremaitre, Cass. crim., July 18, 1851, D.P. 1851. 5. 248, Jour. Pal. 1853. 1. 451; Dareau, Cass. crim., Dec. 23, 1852., D.P. 1853. 5. 215, Jour. Pal. 1853. 2. 525.

[24] D.P. 1927. 4. 265, S. 1927. L. 910.

[25] Lemontey, Du rôle de l'autorité judiciaire dans la procédure d'extradition passive 12 (1966); Mestre, Les traités et le droit interne, 38 Recueil des Cours 233, 268 (1931 IV).

[26] De la Granville, Cass. crim., June 30, 1827, S. 1825-27. 1. 628.

[27] E.g., circular of the Minister of Justice of April 5, 1841, 42 D. Rép. 588.

[28] Dermenon, Cass. crim., Sept. 4, 1840, D.P. 1840. 1. 439, 42 D. Rép. 597. But see, Bastianesi, Cass. crim., July 31, 1845, D.P. 1845. 1. 353.

interpret a treaty of extradition, these cases could not necessarily be applied to other types of treaty, especially those in which the administration did not perform such a vital role in their implementation.[29]

Nevertheless, the characterization of treaties as acts of "high administration" in the 1851 and 1852 extradition cases was a reflection of their ambiguous nature. In order to refute the idea that treaties were simple administrative acts to be interpreted by the administration, the Procureur Général Dupin, in the *Duke of Richmond*, had described treaties as "acts of government and of sovereignty" binding on the courts as are laws. The reality which was reflected by the different terms and their manipulation was that in the interpretation and application of treaties the courts had more potential for interfering with the administration or politics of the state, and in particular the administration of foreign affairs, than they did in most other kinds of cases. This became evident in the next important treaty case in 1861.

The case itself was an insignificant affair involving the estate of an American woman who had died in Paris.[30] The 1788 treaty between France and the United States gave American consuls the right to inventory and seal the assets of the estates of Americans who died in France in the absence of an executor appointed by will, the guardian of a minor or of heirs. In the case at bar the assets of the decedent found in the hospital where she died were placed under seal as a routine matter by the court. The American consul petitioned the court to lift the seals on the grounds that he had sole responsibility for the conservation of the estate. This petition was opposed by a Mme Roode who alleged that she was the heir and that the seals should not be lifted except in her presence.

The lower court held that the grant of authority in the treaty to the American consul to take the inventory and sell the assets also gave him the sole authority to conserve the assets and to proceed to liquidate and distribute the estate. Since Mme Roode was foreigner there was no French interest at stake and no reason for the French courts to intervene in the distribution of the estate.

If Mme Roode had appealed, the court of appeal and eventually the Cour de Cassation could have reversed the decision and the case would probably

[29] In Renneçon, Cass. crim., July 4, 1867, D.P. 1867. 1. 281, the Government insisted upon the discretionary nature of an extradition as the reason why it was impossible for a court to interpret the treaty. In quashing the decision below the Criminal Chamber stated that "treaties... *of extradition* are diplomatic acts from Government to Government which the courts can neither explain nor interpret...." (Emphasis added.)

[30] Trouttman, Cass. req., July 24, 1861, D.P. 1861. 1. 342 (req. Dupin), S. 1861. 1. 687.

have had little impact on the law. However, she did not appeal before the Minister of Justice directed the Procureur Général to file a petition for *excès de pouvoir* in the Cour de Cassation.[31]

The reason for the Government's use of such an extraordinary procedure in the instant case was that the treaty of 1788 had been denounced by the United States in 1798. Since that time French consuls had been refused the right to participate in the distribution of the estates of French citizens who died in the United States. During the negotiations which led to the 1853 consular convention the American authorities had refused to insert any provision respecting the powers of consuls in the distribution of estates. If the trial decision was allowed to stand, the United States would benefit from a right which it had steadfastly refused to grant to France.

The Government's unhappiness, then, was due to the position in which it had been put vis-à-vis the United States, not because a court had exercised authority over a treaty. Nevertheless, the fact that the Procureur Général had been directed to bring the petition for *excès de pouvoir*, which was the only remedy directly available to the Government, caused him to present every conceivable argument that the court had exceeded its powers.

The Procureur Général's main argument was that the 1788 convention no longer existed. He suggested that the court had exceeded its power in one of two ways in order to apply this non-existent convention. The first argument was that the court had interpreted the 1788 convention and a series of subsequent diplomatic acts in such a manner as to find that the convention was still in force. The second argument was that the court had created an entirely new convention between France and the United States, an act which would obviously exceed its powers. If either of these arguments was accepted, the treaty was non-existent and the consul had no authority in respect to the distribution of the estate.

However, the Procureur Général also argued that if the Cour de Cassation found that the convention was still in existence, the trial court had exceeded its power in that it had "impaired the national sovereignty by attributing to a foreign consul the powers of a French judge when the convention only gives him those of a ministerial official."[32] He should have been allowed only to inventory the estate and dispose of its assets if there were no heirs, but it was the responsibility of the French courts to decide whether a claimant was an heir or not.

[31] See text at note 12 *supra*.
[32] D.P. 1861. 1. at 343-44.

The combination of arguments presented by the Procureur Général is a clear indication that the Government was interested only in the result to be achieved, not in the techniques by which that result was achieved. That may also have been the attitude of the Cour de Cassation once it had been assured that the trial court had recognized in the American consul an authority not allowed to French consuls in the United States. Its opinion is ambiguous but it seemed to say that treaties were administrative acts which could be interpreted only by the administrative authorities,[33] a somewhat strange result since the Procureur Général had invited the Cour de Cassation to interpret the treaty itself since the treaty was not clear. In fact the Procureur Général had argued for what he claimed was the proper interpretation of the treaty in the light of various articles of the Civil Code.

If the Cour de Cassation really meant that a treaty was an administrative act, a court which interpreted any treaty would have violated the doctrine of the separation of powers. Not only should the Cour de Cassation have enforced this result on the appeal of a losing party and on the Government's petition for *excès de pouvoir* but the prefect could file a *déclinatoire de conflit* to require that the treaty receive an administrative interpretation.[34]

This procedure was used in 1868, apparently for the first time in respect to treaties.[35] The Conseil d'État, before which the question was raised when the court in which the litigation was in progress refused to dismiss the case,[36] held that it did not violate the separation of powers for the court to interpret a treaty.[37] Although the Conseil d'État did not specifically state that a treaty was not an "administrative act," that was the only logical conclusion. This conclusion was confirmed in 1873 by the Cour de Cassation in so many words.[38] The 1861 decision appeared to be an aberration.

However, it was an aberration only in the choice of the words which had been used by the Cour de Cassation. Governmental dominance in the interpretation of treaties was to come about through another channel, the develop-

[33] "Although the judicial authority can apply administrative acts of which the meaning and the scope are not in doubt to the questions of which it is properly seized and to the facts which attach thereto, it cannot do so when the meaning of these acts is ambiguous..., and this interpretation can only be given by the administrative authority." *Ibid.* at 344.

[34] See text at note 11 *supra*.

[35] Cie générale des asphaltes v. Breittmayer, Conseil d'État, Dec. 12, 1868, D.P. 1869. 3. 59, S. 1869. 2. 307.

[36] Except for a brief period during the Second Republic, prior to 1872 the conflicts were raised to the Conseil d'État. Since 1872 they have gone to the Tribunal des Conflits.

[37] The *déclinatoire de conflit* is available, however, if the court is adjudicating the measures taken by the administration to implement the treaty. Villebrun, Tribunal des Conflits, June 30, 1877, D.P. 1878. 3. 15, S. 1879. 2. 159; Goulet, Tribunal des Conflits, Dec. 14, 1872, D.P. 1873. 3. 10, S. 1873. 2. 124. *La publication des engagements internationaux en France*, [1962] Ann. Fr. Dr. Int'l. 888, 895.

[38] Balestrini v. Aubert, Cass. req., Jan. 6, 1873, D.P. 1873. 1. 116, S. 1873. 1. 24.

ment of the formula first found in the *Duke of Richmond* in 1839 and repeated by the Cour de Cassation in its 1873 decision that treaties "can be applied and even interpreted by the judicial authorities when it is a question of contests having private interests as their object." As in the *Duke of Richmond* the 1873 case involved a matter of private interests and the court went on to interpret the treaty. Finally, in 1877 the Criminal Chamber of the Cour de Cassation relied on a distinction between questions of treaty interpretation involving matters of private interest and questions involving public policy to deny the right of the courts to interpret the treaty before them.[39]

The treaty in question governed the jurisdiction of the French and Spanish courts over the prosecution of smugglers captured with sixteen kilometers of the border. The court of appeal had interpreted the treaty to hold that the French courts had jurisdiction, a result which was possible but which did not arise out of a literal reading of the treaty. On the petition of the defendant the Criminal Chamber quashed the decision on the grounds that the court of appeal had exceeded its powers and violated the doctrine of the separation of powers.

The Criminal Chamber said that although the courts can interpret treaties where such interpretation concerns private interests, "as to all that which concerns questions of public order involving the measures of protection stipulated by the contracting sovereigns in favor of their respective nationals, the diplomatic conventions, being acts of Government to Government, can be interpreted only by the Governments themselves."[40]

The decision followed the recommendation of the *rapporteur* whose discussion of the problem was brief and offered no explanation of the reasons why the courts could not interpret the treaty. He simply informed the Criminal Chamber that the question whether the courts had the authority to interpret treaties had arisen often in matters of extradition, that they had always decided that the courts did not have the authority to interpret treaties and that this treaty was similar to a treaty of extradition. However, he noted that in the *Duke of Richmond* the Civil Chamber recognized the right of the courts to interpret treaties, but only in private matters.

There is always something disquieting to find that the articulated basis for a fundamental decision was an incorrect statement of prior law as it was in this case. It has already been pointed out that the decisions involving treaties of extradition did not arise out of the law of treaties. They were merely applica-

[39] Yter, Cass. crim., July 27, 1877, D.P. 1878. 1. 137 (rapport Gast, note Béquet), S. 1877. 1. 485.

[40] D.P. 1878. 1. at 139, S. 1877. 1. at 486.

tions of the law of extradition. Moreover, the *Duke of Richmond* did not stand for the position that treaties could be interpreted *only* when they involved questions of private interest. The Civil Chamber had held no more than that whenever the courts had jurisdiction of a case, they had the authority to interpret any applicable treaty. The reference to private interests was simply a recognition that the jurisdiction of the Civil Chamber and of the courts over which it presided was restricted to matters of private interest. While this may not have been clear from the language of the Civil Chamber itself, it was absolutely clear in the conclusions of the Procureur Général.

He had begun by acknowledging the principle of the separation of the administrative and judicial powers. However, he stated, treaties are not mere administrative acts. They are of a higher order, namely acts of government and of sovereignty. They are published in the *Bulletin des lois*, have the force of law and "obligate all citizens, as do the laws themselves, and not only those to whom they are addressed or whom they concern, as do administrative acts.... Treaties are placed over all authorities, judicial, administrative or others." Their application and interpretation is to be accomplished by whichever authority has jurisdiction over the problem.

Execution belongs to the diplomats when a principal treaty requires accessory conventions....

Execution can be confided to the army, if it cannot be obtained otherwise....

Execution will be political if it is a treaty of alliance or an act of mediation. It can require the cooperation of the administration if the acts are within its jurisdiction.

But it must also be admitted that the judicial authority has its share of attributions in the execution of treaties, if there arise private disputes which fall within their competence, such as questions of property, family, succession or others of this sort. In all these cases, a recourse to the courts of the country is necessary, a recourse which is sometimes indicated by the treaty itself, but which, in case of silence on this point, is none the less a necessity of law, if such should be the case.

In these different cases, the interpretation and the application of treaties devolve on each authority to be exercised by it in its own manner.[41]

The Procureur Général went on to point out that France had discharged its political obligations under the treaty by lifting the sequestration to Aubigny and by rendering the property to the Fourth Duke of Richmond. The dispute was strictly between the private parties and, as between them, was "a petition of inheritance, an action for partition, a debate over property. The court must thus decide on the law and the quality of the parties; it must not leave the

[41] Jour. Pal. 1839. 2. at 212-13.

title to the property uncertain."[42] He closed by saying that the state had no interest in the outcome of the dispute. It claimed no title and it had given no guarantee to the Duke of Richmond.

If the state had claimed title to Aubigny or had given a guarantee of title, the consequences for the jurisdiction of the courts would have gone beyond any question of the interpretation of the treaty. The Prefectural Council, which was the local administrative tribunal, had jurisdiction over all contests to the title to land sold as part of the national domain, in which case the state had given the buyer a guarantee of title, or which was claimed by the state or other governmental entity. These rules of jurisdiction applied whether or not there was a treaty involved in the case.[43]

Even though the references to the *Duke of Richmond* and to the extradition cases were not an historically accurate justification for the distinction between questions of private interest and questions of public order which was drawn by the Criminal Chamber in 1877, the distinction reflected sound public policy as it was perceived in France. The courts could interpret the treaty in the vast bulk of cases which came before them in which neither the foreign nor the French Government had any substantial interest. Where there did seem to be a substantial impact on foreign affairs, the courts could solicit an interpretation of the treaty from the Government.

Although the private interest/public order distinction was quickly accepted as the correct statement of the law by the civil courts as well as by the criminal courts, there were in fact relatively few reported cases prior to 1920, other than those involving extradition, in which a court solicited an interpretation and even fewer in which the Cour de Cassation quashed the decision below for a failure to do so.[44] Even such matters as the nationality of a person, which would seem to be the quintescence of a question of public order, was seen as matter of private interest because it resulted in the determination of his civil status.[45] Nevertheless, the verbal distinction became well established and treaties which were interpreted by the courts raised – by definition – questions of a private interest only.

A problem which was unresolved by the Criminal Chamber in 1877 was who had the authority to interpret the treaty when the courts did not. The Criminal Chamber had said that "diplomatic conventions, being acts of

[42] *Ibid.* at 213.

[43] Law of 28 Pluviôse an 8 (Feb. 17, 1800), art. 4. Compare Féry v. Préfet du Pas-de-Calais, Cour royale de Douai, March 8, 1841, 10 D. Rép. 439, with Hospices de Béthune v. Goudenmetz, Cour royale de Douai, Jan. 2, 1843, 42 D. Rép. 560.

[44] See Appert, *De l'interprétation des traités diplomatiques au cours d'un procès*, 26 Clunet 433 (1899).

[45] *Ibid.* at 435-36.

Government to Government, can be interpreted only by the Governments themselves."[46] The commentator to the case noted that this was because the interpretation of the treaty by one of the states would violate the sovereignty of the other state. If this was the rationale on which the doctrine rested, the Criminal Chamber's statement that there had been a violation of the separation of powers meant that the lower court had exercised a power which lay in part in the foreign Government. The only acceptable interpretation would have to come from the joint action of the two states. For understandable reasons this was not insisted upon by the courts, but it was not exactly clear why the courts should follow the Government's interpretation rather than its own if a bilateral interpretation was not available.

Self-Execution and Supremacy

The question whether a treaty could be self-executing in a dispute which arose in the courts has not been a pressing problem. As was stated above neither the pre-Revolutionary nor the post-Revolutionary courts had any serious difficulty in enforcing treaties once they were published, and sometimes even though the clause remained unpublished.[47]

The argument that a treaty was an executive act over which the courts should have limited authority because of the separation of powers was directed only at the question of who should interpret the treaty, not whether it was self-executing. That was true whether the argument was raised by the defendant, the prefect, the Procureur Général on orders from the Minister of Justice, or the court itself.

Nor does the argument seem to have been raised at any time that treaties in general were not enforceable in the courts because of the lack of legislative approval.[48] Many executive acts were enforceable in the courts. Not only does the Government have the authority to issue the regulations necessary to implement legislation, but throughout every regime the Government has had a limited independent law making capacity.[49] It was not an unusual

[46] Yter, Cass. crim., July 27, 1877, D.P. 1878. 1. 137 (rapport Gast, note Béquet), S. 1877. 1. 485.

[47] The specific treaty provision in question in the *Duke of Richmond* was never published officially. However, the requirement that the treaty be published before it was binding on the courts was established in Jauge, Cass. crim., Nov. 28, 1834, S. 1834. 1. 822. But see Baranez v. Crédit du Nord, Cour d'appel de Paris, March 18, 1969, J.C.P. 1969. II. 15875 (note P.L.), 97 Clunet 66 (note Ruzié) (1970), in which the court of appeal suspended its proceedings in order to request a copy of a secret agreement with Algeria from the Minister of Foreign Affairs.

[48] However, in 1826 the Government, which had signed a treaty of navigation with Great Britain and declared it in force by an executive act was forced to submit it for parliamentary approval. Demangeat, *Les dispositions des différents Codes ne peuvent-elles être modifiées que par une Loi, et non par un Traité diplomatique?*, 1 Clunet 107, 109 (1874).

[49] See generally, Sieghart, Government by Decree 252-305 (1950).

situation, therefore, for the courts to enforce "law" created by the executive. Since the executive was authorized to conclude treaties, it was accepted as a matter of course that the courts would enforce them.

While the re-establishment of legislative supremacy in 1871 raised some question about the earlier treaties which had been adopted by the Emperor alone,[50] the courts eventually recognized their enforceability. The considerations were perhaps more in the area of practical politics than of legal or constitutional theory. It was feared in the basic case that the failure to recognize the rights of a Italian national under the 1862 copyright convention with Italy would undoubtedly lead to the withdrawal by Italy of the rights of French nationals under the treaty.[51] Any impediment to the republican doctrine of legislative supremacy which might result from the enforcement of the treaty was no more serious than that which resulted from the continued validity of imperial decrees and ordonnances.

The question of supremacy between treaty and statute was also not of importance prior to 1920 even though it was potentially present every time a treaty was enforced by a court. No reported cases recognized it as a problem until after the fall of the Second Empire. Statements such as Merlin's in 1811 that the "treaty of January 11, 1787 was a law for France"[52] and that of the Cour de Cassation in the *Duke of Richmond* that treaties "have the character of law" were sufficient to cause the courts automatically to resolve any incipient conflicts through the use of the techniques of statutory construction.

Since those treaties which had some domestic effect were almost always both bilateral and on narrow subjects, two separate but allied techniques of statutory construction were applicable. The first was that special statutes in derogation of the general rule are construed narrowly, the functional equivalent of the American rule that statutes in derogation of the common law are construed narrowly. In the context of treaties this meant that any ambiguity in meaning was resolved in favor of an interpretation in conformity with the prevailing French law.[53] This approach was most obvious in the *Duke of Richmond* in which the Cour de Cassation applied the French law of succession since it was "impossible to believe that the intention of the plenipoten-

[50] In the decision of Feb. 5, 1874, Tribunal de la Seine, 1 Clunet 107 (1874) (note Demangeat), the court held that the 1862 consular convention with Spain was unenforceable for lack of parliamentary approval. It was said in the accompanying note to have been the only such holding to that time.

[51] Grus v. Ricordi, Cass. req., July 25, 1887, D.P. 1888. 1. 5 (concl. Lepelletier, note Sarrut), S. 1888. 1. 17 (note Lyon-Caen).

[52] Text at note 15 *supra*.

[53] 1 Bartin, Principes de droit international privé ¶ 53 (1930); Battifol, Droit international privé ¶ 38 (4e éd. 1967).

tiaries [who negotiated the treaty] had intended to regulate the rights between coheirs."[54] The result was more important in such treaties as the Franco-Swiss treaties of 1828 and 1867 on the jurisdiction of courts in which there are divergencies between the interpretations given the treaty by the French and the Swiss courts, almost always in the direction of the respective domestic law.[55]

Since treaties were interpreted narrowly and in conformity with French law wherever possible, the second rule of statutory construction could be applied. Treaties were considered to be exceptions to the otherwise applicable statute. No problem of supremacy arose. It was merely a question of applying the appropriate norm where two were available. There was no need even to apply the rule that the later in time of two conflicting statutes governs the earlier.

THE LEASE LEGISLATION CONFRONTATION 1914 TO 1950

Condition of Foreigners in France

When the confrontation came which destroyed the smooth working relationship between treaty and statute it was not because of a change in the actions of the courts, nor was it the result of a change in the policy of the Government. It was the result of a change in the treatment of foreigners under French domestic legislation.

Prior to 1914 there were few distinctions between the rights of French and foreign nationals.[56] The Revolution of 1789 had proclaimed the brotherhood of man and ended the few restrictions on foreigners which still existed at the end of the *ancien régime*. Unfortunately, the brotherhood of man did not long survive in an unadulterated form. The nationalism which arose during the long years of war beginning in 1792 and the desire for some diplomatic bargaining tools to improve the lot of the French citizens living abroad combined to introduce some new restrictions in the Civil Code when it was adopted in 1804.

[54] Jour. Pal. 1839. 2. at 219.

[55] Flattet, *Un traité centenaire: La Convention franco-suisse du 15 juin 1869 sur la compétence judiciaire et l'exécution des jugements*, 58 Rev. Cr. D.I.P. 577 (1969).

[56] There is an extensive bibliography on the condition of foreigners in France. The best current source is Simon-Depitre, *Conditions des étrangers en France*, Juris-Classeur, Droit International, fascs. 523, 525-A, 525-B and 525-C (1960 with *mise à jour*). The history of the condition of foreigners is described in fasc. 523. Although it is quickly going out of date, Simon-Depitre, L'activité professionelle des étrangers en France (1955), is valuable for restrictions on the commercial activities of foreigners.

The fundamental provision was found in article 11.

> The foreigner enjoys the same *droits civils* in France as those which are or will be accorded to French nationals by treaties of the nation to which the foreigner belongs.

In addition to article 11 there were two specific restrictions. One prevented a foreigner from receiving property either by will, by intestate succession or by gift.[57] This restriction was removed by the law of July 14, 1819. The law substituted certain benefits for the French heir, a provision which has caused problems ever since.[58] The second specific restriction found in the Civil Code was the requirement that a foreigner put up a bond to cover the costs of litigation should he lose the action, the *caution judicatum solvi*, a bond not required of French plaintiffs.[59]

Although the specific restrictions on foreigners were important and a number of treaties have been negotiated to eliminate their application, the history of the legal rights of foreigners in France has been bound up in the interpretation of article 11. Article 11 was never simply a restrictive provision. When measured against the restrictions on foreigners which had been in force during the Middle Ages and which were still part of the knowledge of the legal world of 1804, article 11 was an extremely liberal provision. A foreigner could exercise any *droit civil* in France which his country would grant by treaty to a French citizen. Only the political rights were excluded. If everything worked as it was hoped, not only France but all other countries would grant the full enjoyment of all *droits civils* to all foreigners.

Naturally, all the hoped for treaties were not negotiated and it was necessary to interpret article 11 to determine the rights of foreigners absent a treaty. From a strict reading such foreigners had no rights. It was obvious, however, that an exception had to be implied for those few rights specifically granted to foreigners by other articles of the Civil Code or other statutes. Even as modified this strict interpretation was impractical. There were few statutes which either specifically included or specifically excluded foreign nationals from their operation. Those who advocated a strict approach found it necessary as a practical matter to interpret the statutes which did not specifically grant rights to foreign nationals in an extremely broad fashion.

[57] C. Civ., arts. 726 and 912.

[58] S. 1789-1830. L. 1013. For a reaction to the impact of the law of July 14, 1819, on Franco-American legal relations, Delaume, American-French Private International Law 40-44 (2nd ed. 1961).

[59] C. Civ., art. 16.

For example, Demolombe drew from the combination of articles 3, 14 and 15 of the Civil Code the conclusion that foreign nationals has been granted

> The concession of all *droits civils* by means of which property in goods is acquired and transmitted, by means of which claims are created and extinguished, as well as well as all the *droits civils* relative to the proof ... of the different events by which property is acquired or alienated, by which claims are contracted or extinguished.[60]

As a result the theoretically strict approach that foreign nationals have no legal rights except those specifically granted ended with a broad catalog of implied rights. However, it was an awkward technique. Since the exegetic process required some legislative basis from which to begin, the result was uneven. The accidents of legislative drafting determined whether foreign nationals were recognized as enjoying broad categories of rights.

A second interpretation of article 11 began from the opposite position from that of the first. Foreign nationals should have all rights created by law unless the statute specifically excluded them from its operation.[61] As a practical matter this eliminated the effect of article 11, except to affirm that any specific restriction on the *droits civils* of foreigners could be lifted by treaty, a proposition about which there was no doubt in 1804. It is by far the most liberal interpretation of article 11, the one which is the easiest to administer, and the one in favor today.[62] However, its liberalism in practice is dependent upon the absence of legislation restricting foreigners from enjoying specific legal rights.

Although each of these two interpretations of article 11 had some support among the writers and the courts, a third interpretation based upon the ancient distinction between those legal rights created by the *jus gentium*, now generally called the *droit des gens*, and those created by the *droit civil* carried the day throughout the latter part of the nineteenth and the first part of the twentieth century. *Droits civils*, under this theory, comprised the legal rights created by the civil law of a given state whereas the *jus gentium* referred to all those "facilities and advantages which [are] generally envisaged by the different civilized nations as flowing from natural law or which [are] generally found in fact in their legislation...."[63] Those legal rights which were a part of the *jus gentium* were of right granted to foreign nationals; the legal rights

[60] 1 Demolombe, Cours de Code Napoléon ¶ 243 (3e éd. 1865).

[61] Demangeat, Histoire de la condition civile des étrangers en France dans l'ancien et le nouveau droit ¶ 56 (1844); Vallette, Explication sommaire du Livre Ier du Code Napoléon et des lois accessoires 407 (1859), as cited in Simon-Depitre, *Condition des étrangers*, fasc. 523, ¶ 82.

[62] Battifol, Droit international privé ¶ 177.

[63] 1 Aubry et Rau, Cours de droit civil français ¶ 78 (5e éd. by Rau et Falcimaigne 1897).

which were based on the *droit civil* were available to foreign nationals only if the law so authorized.

The categorization of legal rights into those recognized by the *jus gentium* and those created by the *droit civil* was not very satisfactory. It was not possible to rely upon either the classifications of the Roman law or the classifications which had been developed during the *ancien régime*, both of which had served other purposes. Moreover, every legal institution partook of both the *jus gentium* in the human need which was fulfilled and of the *droit civil* in respect to the particular means by which it was accomplished.[64]

As a practical matter the tenants of this theory found relatively few legal rights which had been created by the *droit civil.* Aubry and Rau, who were the principle proponents of the theory, listed as *droits civils* from which foreigners were excluded only the right of the father and mother to the income of a minor child, the right to adopt, the right to trade marks and trade names and the right of married women, minor children, and legal incompetents to an *hypothèque légale.*[65] None of these *droits civils* was of great practical significance at the time, though trade marks and trade names became so later.

During the nineteenth century the controversy was over technique and verbal formulations, not primarily over substance. So long as there were few statutes which denied foreigners legal rights granted to French citizens, all three theories produced the same general result. It was in commerce that the assimilation of foreign nationals to French nationals was most important. As late as 1908 Weiss wrote in his treatise on Private International Law that

> If there is a natural right for a man after that of living, it is assuredly that to seek in his work, in the exercise of commerce, of industry or in any profession whatever the resources indispensable to his subsistence and to that of his family.
>
> This right belongs to all foreigners in France, as it belongs to all French. It could not, without an odious tyranny, be entirely refused to them. One must condemn in principle the obstacles which have been caused them by vexacious regulations or discriminatory taxes.[66]

In view of the liberal interpretation of article 11 which resulted from all three theories and from the work of the courts, it is surprising to find that the courts interpreted article 11 very strictly when it came to the determination whether a treaty relieved a foreigner of one of the few restrictions imposed upon him. They demanded that the right which French citizens could enjoy

[64] Battifol, Droit international privé ¶ 177.
[65] Aubry et Rau, note 63 *supra.*
[66] Weiss, Traité théorique et pratique de droit international privé 127 (2e éd. 1908).

in the foreign country as a result of the treaty be exactly the same as that in question in France. This posed no problem for treaties dispensing with the *caution judicatum solvi,* because in both countries nationals of the other country could bring civil actions on the same basis as the domestic nationals.[67] However, it was more difficult when the foreign substantive law which the treaty made available to French citizens did not have the same legal consequences as the French substantive law. In the most often cited case which illustrates the difficulty the Cour de Cassation held that a Swiss woman from the canton of Vaud could not receive the benefit of the *hypothèque légale.*[68] Whereas the *hypothèque légale* in France arose as of right and covered all of the community property, the system for the protection of the wife's share in the community property under the Civil Code of Vaud had to be consented to by the husband within a certain period of time by certain formalities and was limited to the real property on which it had been given. Since the two rights were not rigorously the same, article 11 precluded the plaintiff from the benefit of the *hypothèque légale.* In order for a foreigner to exercise one of the few *droits civils* from which he was barred by article 11, there had to be both treaty and legislative reciprocity.

Rent Control Legislation

The practical identity of the legal rights of foreigners and French citizens lasted until World War I. Upon the outbreak of the war a temporary moratorium was enacted suspending the due dates of all civil and commercial obligations, including those due under leases of real property.[69] The moratorium was continued with modifications throughout the war. In its original form it was presumably applicable to everyone in France, since it did not mention either those covered or those excluded from its effects. However, it was soon specifically extended to the subjects of all allied and neutral states as well as to those Poles, Czechs and inhabitants of Alsace and Lorraine who had received a resident permit.[70] Only enemy aliens not named in the decree were in fact excluded from its benefits.

[67] Simon-Depitre, *Caution "judicatum solvi"*, Juris-Classeur, Droit International, fasc. 589-A,

[68] Monnet v. Pinget, Cass. req., Jan. 27, 1903, D.P. 1903. 1. 249 (rapport George-Lemaire. note E.L.), S. 1904. 1. 81 (note Pillet).

An *hypothèque légale* is the security interest of a married woman, minor child or legal incompetent in the real property of a decendent to guarantee any claims against the succession.

[69] Decree of Aug. 14, 1914, J.O. Aug. 15, 1914, D.P. 1914. 4. 91, authorized by law of Aug. 5, 1914, J.O. Aug. 6, 1914, D.P. 1914. 4. 88.

[70] Decree of Dec. 17, 1914, J.O. Dec. 18, 1914, D.P. 1915. 4. 43.

In March 1918 the inflation and the shortage of housing caused by the great destruction in northern France led to the enactment of a separate rent control law.[71] The law introduced such provisions as the tenant's right to have his rent reduced under certain circumstances, his right to extend an expired lease and the landlord's overriding right to repossess the property at the expiration of a lease for his personal or family use. In the original bill the benefits of the law were again to be extended to essentially all but enemy aliens, this time on a basis of reciprocity, but by the time the bill was enacted they were limited to French nationals, inhabitants of the French protectorates and of the lost territories in Alsace and Lorraine, and to nationals of those states allied with France in the war.[72] In addition the President, acting on the recommendation of the Minister of Foreign Affairs, was given the authority to extend by decree the benefits of the statute to the nationals of other states.

The decree which followed in August 1918[73] implemented the will of the Parliament, as it was understood by the Government, "to reduce as much as possible the money burden imposed by the war on those who on the side of the *entente* had borne the sorrow, the perils and the losses which it had caused all the French"[74] by extending most of the benefit of the law to (1) those individuals who had served in the French or allied armies, even though neither a French nor an allied national, (2) the "nationalities oppressed by the enemy," i.e., the minority groups within the German, Austro-Hungarian and Ottoman empires, (3) Russians, (4) Monagasques and, (5) all other non-enemy aliens who had suffered pecuniary loss as a result of the hostilities.

The 1918 law and its implementation by the decree were not anti-foreign. However, it was clear that the general mood of the country had changed from that prevailing in 1914. While France was still open to foreigners, it now seemed only fair that special benefits like those which arose out of the rent control legislation should be reserved for those foreigners who could claim the sympathy of the French. Although the class of foreigners who could claim the sympathy of the French was broadly defined, a major new category of legal rights was denied to at least some foreign nationals.

Between 1918 and 1926 other statutes were passed governing in some way or another the status of leased property and in each case some restriction was introduced on its applicability to foreigners. It had been recognized that

[71] Law of March 9, 1918, J.O. March 12, 1918, D.P. 1918. 4. 49.
[72] Art. 62. The legislative history of article 62 is set out in a note in D.P. 1918. 4. at 131.
[73] Decree of Aug. 29, 1918, J.O. Aug. 31, 1918, D.P. 1918. 4. 226.
[74] Circular from the Minister of Justice of Aug. 30, 1918, J.O. Aug. 31, 1918, D.P. 1918. 4. 226.

the right to extend a lease, a necessary corollary to any rent control legislation, was a serious interference with the right of property. It did not seem proper to subject French landlords to such an extraordinary interference with their property rights at the instance of foreigners generally. On the other hand it was thought unconscionable that a foreign landlord should be able to dispossess a French tenant during an acute housing shortage, even if the lease had expired and the foreign landlord intended to use the property for his personal or family use.[75]

The *mélange* of rules arising out of the numerous statutes was replaced in 1926 by two new statutes, one covering leases of dwellings[76] and the second covering leases of commercial property.[77] These two statutes remained in effect until the advent of World War II in 1939 and they continue to influence the legislation which is currently in force.

The housing statute of April 1, 1926 remained what it had been since 1914, a temporary law enacted for social purposes during a period when there was both inflation and a housing shortage. Then as now, it was official policy to encourage the construction of sufficient housing to eliminate any need for the legislation.

The statute on commercial leases of June 30, 1926 fulfilled an entirely different purpose. It filled a gap in the definition of the *fonds de commerce* as that term was described in the law of March 17, 1909.[78] The term *fonds de commerce* describes a business as an entity. One of its elements is the goodwill of the firm's clientele. The clientele was understood to comprise two groups of customers, those who are attracted by the establishment's good name, and those who are attracted by the establishment's location. The establishment's name was already protected by the legislation on trade names, but with no right to renew a lease the value of the *fonds de commerce* attributable to the location diminished constantly as the expiration of the lease approached. The primary function of the law of June 30, 1926, was to grant merchants the right to extend their lease so as to protect their interest in the clientele.[79] As a corollary, it was necessary to provide the mechanism for adjusting the rent for the extended lease period.

The result of the two statutes was essentially the same. In both cases there

[75] These points were particularly evident in the debates over the law of Aug. 2, 1924, J.O. Aug. 3, 1924, D.P. 1925. 4. 24, which is excerpted in D.P. 1925. 4. at 32-33.

[76] Law of April 1, 1926, J.O. April 2, 1926, D.P. 1926. 4. 113.

[77] Law of June 30, 1926, J.O. July 1, 1926, D.P. 1926, D.P. 1926. 4. 257.

[78] Law of March 17, 1909, art. 9, J.O. March 19, 1909, D.P. 1909. 4. 41.

[79] The statute was primarily designed to protect small family owned businesses. In that respect it had much in common with the law of April 1, 1926, covering the leases of dwellings.

was a right of extension on the part of the lessee, a right to retake the property by the landlord for his own purposes, and a mechanism for an adjustment of the rent. However, the fact that the statute on commercial leases was not formally a rent control statute was to have some consequences at a later time.

There was no distinction between French citizens and foreigners in the housing bill when it was introduced by the Government. Experience had shown that a foreigner who had no right to extend his lease was a particularly desirable tenant to the detriment of potential French lessees. Nevertheless, the Parliament excluded all foreign lessees from the right to extend a lease except (1) those who had served in the French, allied or associated armies, or whose sons or sons-in-law had so served, (2) nationals of protected or mandated states, (3) those who had been "admitted to domicile" in France, and (4) those whose children were French.[80] The law also provided that the exclusion of foreign lessees from the right to extend a lease was "subject to the treaties existing on the day of the promulgation of the present law," i.e. April 1, 1926. It was quickly pointed out that by necessity the statute was also subject to treaties subsequently adopted and the reference to treaties was removed in 1929.[81] The owner's right to retake property for his personal or family use on the termination of a lease was restricted even further; it was available only to French nationals.[82]

The commercial lease statute also began with the fundamental principle of excluding all foreigners from the benefit of its provisions with exceptions similar to those in the housing lease statute.[83] However, where the housing lease statute originally granted its benefits to those foreign lessees whose country had previously entered into treaties with France, the commercial lease statute granted its benefits to foreign lessees only if there was "analogous legislation" in their country available to French nationals. While it was not clear to the Parliament whether any other country had created a property right to extend a commercial lease so as to protect the *fonds de commerce*, such legislation was conceivable in the future.[84]

[80] Art. 4.
[81] Law of June 29, 1929, J.O. June 30, 1929, D.P. 1929. 4. 241.
[82] Art. 5.
[83] Law of June 30, 1926, art. 19, J.O. July 1, 1926, D.P. 1926. 4. 257.
[84] See the legislative history excerpted in D.P. 1926. 4. at 291. The exclusion originally operated only against those foreigners who had acquired their leases prior to January 1, 1923. This strange provision was due to the fact that during the war when the Germans were able to shell Paris itself, there was a shortage of commercial tenants and many foreigners looking for a bargain signed long term leases. Since the passage of time would have eliminated all such leases, eventually the exclusion of foreigners would have constituted merely a principle not realized in practice. However, article 19 was amended by the law of April 22, 1927, art. 11, J.O. April 24, 1927, D.P. 1927. 4. 297, to eliminate the reference to any date.

Litigation

Litigation over the application of the moratorium legislation to foreigners had begun upon its enactment in 1914. Although the early cases concentrated on the question whether various foreigners fell within the enumerated categories, by 1926 it had become clear that the major factor to be considered was the compatibility of the exclusion of foreigners with the obligations France had undertaken by treaty.

Depending on the country foreign litigants and their Governments relied on treaties of Establishment, treaties of Friendship, Commerce and Navigation and on Consular Conventions to claim that France was required to grant them the same rights as French citizens under the lease statutes. The majority of these treaties dated from the mid-nineteenth century and reflected the concerns and the attitudes of the time. They all had the same basic purpose, to facilitate commercial activities between the two states. Their most important function was to assure one signatory state that the other state would not enter into discriminatory tariff arrangements with third states, an assurance sanctioned by a most-favored-nation clause.

In addition, the treaties guaranteed the nationals of each state the right to live in the other, engage in business, own property, sue in the courts, etc. In some treaties the legal rights of the nationals of each state in the other state were listed in some detail. In other treaties the nationals of each state were "assimilated" in general terms to the nationals of the host state. In yet other treaties nationals of one state were granted most-favored-nation status in the second state, a status which automatically became that of an "assimilated" foreigner because of the existence of assimilation clauses in earlier treaties. Whatever their specific wording and scope, they reinforced the prevailing nineteenth century philosophy of a *laissez-faire* society in which government restrictions were reduced to a minimum, particularly on commercial activities. While included as a standard part of all such treaties, the clauses relating to the rights of foreign nationals were of minimal practical importance at the time the treaties were negotiated, since they usually reinforced rights already available under national law.

These treaties had been the subject of some prior litigation, not only in respect to article 11 of the Civil Code but also in respect to the relatively few specific statutes which had differentiated between French citizens and foreigners. The courts had treated both kinds of restrictions in the same way. They were applied to foreigners unless there was both treaty and legislative reciprocity which gave French citizens the same rights in the foreign country that the foreigner was claiming in France, reciprocity *trait pour trait* as it was called by Niboyet.[85] These cases obviously constituted a precedent for the means by which the lease cases should be decided.

However, there was a significant difference between the prior litigation and that conducted in respect to the lease legislation. The prior cases had been episodic and concerned matters of relative unimportance either to France or to the foreign states whose nationals were involved. The foreign states had not been sufficiently concerned to register any significant protest on those occasions when their citizens were given less than national treatment in France.

The controversy over the lease legislation could not have differed more. The rights in question were of great importance. The shortage of housing and commercial property caused by the war had never been alleviated and it was of great significance whether a lessee could extend a lease or a landlord retake the property for his personal or family use. Secondly, the legislative intent to exclude most foreigners had become quite clear over the years. The Parliament had consistently resisted the efforts of the Ministry of Foreign Affairs to treat foreigners the same as French in this legislation. Thirdly, the legislation affected large numbers of foreigners. France has traditionally been a country which has welcomed foreigners as permanent residents but which has restricted the right to acquire French citizenship. Every one of these thousands of foreign residents, many of whom had lived in France for long periods of time, was potentially affected by the legislation.[86] Not many were in a position to claim an *hypothèque légale*, but most had a lease on their apartment, some on their commercial property, and a few owned property which they now could not repossess at the expiration of a lease. Fourthly, France had a treaty with some form of an assimilation or most-favored-nation clause with almost every state from which significant numbers of foreign residents living in France had come. If the treaties required national treatment, the parliamentary effort to restrict the benefit of the legislation to French citizens and those who had a special claim on France arising out of wartime service or family relations would have been effectively negated. Fifthly, many foreigners were claiming their rights in litigation under the statutes and the treaties. This flood of litigation involving different rights under different statutes and alleging different treaties changed the focus of

[85] Niboyet, *La notion de réciprocité dans les traités diplomatiques de droit international privé*, 52 Recueil des Cours 253, 297 (1935 II).

[86] In the original text of both the law of April 1, 1926 and of the law of June 30, 1926 there was an exception made for foreigners who had been admitted to domicile. However, the provisions in the Civil Code relevant to the admission to domicile were repealed by the law of Aug. 10, 1927, art. 13, J.O. Aug. 14, 1927, D.P. 1928. 4. 1.

For some figures on the number of foreigners resident in France, see note 119 *infra*.

attention from the rights of any given foreigner derived by an exegesis of statute and treaty to a broader discussion of the rights of foreigners in general. While some cases were decided on the basis of the differences in wording of statute or treaty or on the existence of "analogous legislation" in the foreigner's home country, it was soon evident that a global answer covering at least most of the cases would be necessary. Sixthly, the practical consequences were too important for either the foreign governments or the French Ministry of Foreign Affairs to remain indifferent to the outcome.

In spite of the differences between the lease controversy and the earlier disputes involving treaties, the courts generally followed the techniques which they had always used. The first step was to interpret the statute and determine whether the foreigner could claim rights directly under it. This led to a few decisions in favor of foreigners.[87] If the foreigner could not prevail under the statute, the second step was to interpret the treaty to determine whether it applied to the kind of restriction under consideration. It was only after the treaty had been determined applicable that it was necessary to determine whether there was also legislative reciprocity, the third step in the process.

The majority of the decisions prior to 1929 refused the benefit of the lease statutes to foreigners. Some of the decisions in respect to the lease of dwellings interpreted the treaty as applicable only to the rights of merchants in their commercial capacity.[88] This argument, of course, was not available in respect to commercial leases.

The argument most often relied upon by the courts was that the statutes and treaties had to be interpreted in the light of article 11 of the Civil Code, which required legislative reciprocity.[89] It was understood that the Government could conclude treaties with other states which granted the foreigners national rights. However, the courts generally stated that the treaties would have to refer specifically to the right in question, i.e. to the lessee's right to extend a lease or to the landlord's right to repossess the property on the termination of the lease in the face of the lessee's right to extend it.[90] A variation to the argument was that the treaty was intended only to cover rights arising out of the *jus gentium* and not those created by the *droit civil strictu sensu*, which both the right to extend and the right to repossess were said to be.[91]

[87] E.g., Société générale des transports maritimes à vapeur v. Pellegrini, Cass. req., Jan. 28, 1930, D.H. 1930. 195, S. 1930. 1. 139.
[88] Bazin v. Weatherby, Comm. sup. cass., May 30, 1927, D.H. 1927. 435.
[89] E.g., Pigois v. Corrodi, Comm. sup. cass., Dec. 29, 1927, D.H. 1928. 87; L v. Société X, Cour d'appel de Rennes, June 16, 1930, D.P. 1931. 2. 9 (note Chauveau).
[90] Société immobilière Micheline v. Fischer, Comm. sup. cass., Aug. 1, 1927, D.H. 1927. 483.
[91] *Ibid.*

Although the Ministry of Foreign Affairs had consistently argued that the benefits of the legislation should be extended to all foreigners, as late as 1927 in a response to a parliamentary question it took the position that it could not state whether the treaties affected the application of the lease laws without impinging on the authority of the courts.[92] However, by 1929 the pressures from the foreign governments had grown to the point that it was necessary to act.

The Ministry of Foreign Affairs had in theory three procedures available by which it could have caused the Government to intervene in one of the private cases before the courts. The Minister could have urged his colleague the Minister of the Interior to direct a prefect to file a *déclinatoire de conflit* before one of the trial courts alleging that the treaties raised questions of public order which required an interpretation by an administrative authority. Secondly, the Minister could have urged his colleague the Minister of Justice to direct the Procureur Général to file a petition for *excès de pouvoir* with the Cour de Cassation alleging either that an improper interpretation had been given[93] or that the lower court had not had the authority to interpret the treaty. Thirdly, the Minister could have requested the Minister of Justice to have his interpretation of the treaty transmitted to the court by the appropriate *procureur*.

The problem with all of these procedures was that they relied upon the good graces of other ministries. The Minister of Justice had already demonstrated his lack of enthusiasm for the concerns of the Minister of Foreign Affairs,[94] the Procureur Général was to do so publicly in 1931[95] and it can be assumed that the Minister of the Interior was not primarily concerned with helping foreigners overcome the restrictive language of the statutes. Moreover, both procedures resulted in the decision of a court and even the Cour de Cassation was untrustworthy from the viewpoint of the Minister of Foreign Affairs.

The Minister of Foreign Affairs turned, therefore, to the one procedure available which did not require the aid of any other ministry. He exchanged letters with Great Britain and Switzerland which interpreted the treaties, caused those letters to be published in the Official Journal and caused to be

[92] Response to Parliamentary question, March 31, 1927, 54 Clunet 776 (1927).

[93] This procedure was used in Pick v. Bernheim, Cass. req., Feb. 5, 1936, S. 1936. 1. 151, to annul the decision of a trial court which had misinterpreted a treaty and thereby failed to apply it.

[94] Mazeaud, Note to Reynes v. Société française des Nouvelles Galeries réunies, Cass. civ., Feb. 24, 1932, S. 1932. 1. 249.

[95] Text at note 102 *infra*.

published a circular addressed to the Minister of Justice in which he justified his authority to conclude definitive interpretations of a treaty.[96]

The interpretative letters used all but identical language. These letters stated the following common understanding: (1) a most-favored-nation clause guaranteed to British and Swiss nationals rights equal to those granted under treaties which assimilated the foreign national to a French national; (2) foreigners who can rely upon an assimilation clause in a treaty have the same rights as French nationals under both lease statutes; and (3) this is so notwithstanding article 11 of the Civil Code.

In this circular addressed to the Minister of Justice the Minister of Foreign Affairs agreed that the courts have the duty to interpret treaties which come before them in the course of litigation. He said, however, that once a dispute arose between the two states over the proper interpretation of a treaty, it is the responsibility of the Governments to determine the proper interpretation whether the provision in question is of public law or of private law. It is not necessary that the interpretation take the form of a formal bilateral agreement. The Minister of Foreign Affairs of one of the two states could recognize the error of the courts to which his attention had been called and rectify it on his own initiative. Anytime there is a diplomatic dispute, the Minister of Foreign Affairs has the authority to intervene. Whenever he officially declares the meaning of a treaty in the name of the Government, his interpretation becomes a part of the treaty and is binding on the courts as it is upon the administration. The treaty is the law of the two states and just as two private parties can determine the meaning of a contract they have passed between them, so it is the right of the two states to determine the meaning of a clause in an agreement between them.

The Minister of Foreign Affairs went on to say that whenever a treaty assimilates a foreigner to a French citizen, there is no question of determining whether French citizens have reciprocal rights in the other country. It is up to the Government to worry whether the treaty rights and obligations are fairly balanced and to denounce the treaty when they no longer are.

Neither article 11 of the Civil Code nor any of the provisions in the two lease statutes "can defeat an assimilation clause. These legal provisions must be understood as excluding all foreigners with the exception of those who are assimilated to Frenchmen."

As a final matter the circular listed nine treaties which he stated contained assimilation clauses granting to the nationals of those states the same rights

[96] Exchange of letters with Great Britain, May 21-25, 1929, J.O. July 20, 1929, S. 1929. L. 2308; Exchange of Letters with Switzerland, July 11-26, 1929, J.O. Aug. 5-6, 1929, S. 1929. L. 2308; Circular, July 22, 1929, J.O. Aug. 12-13, 1929, S. 1929. L. 2308.

under the lease statutes as French nationals could exercise. It listed another twenty-four treaties with most-favored-nation clauses which granted the same rights by reference.

Less than three months later Commission Supérieure de Cassation, the special supreme tribunal for rent control cases, reversed its prior line of authority which had consistently refused to apply the treaties and cited the circular as the basis for holding that the assimilation clause in the Franco-Spanish treaty of 1862 authorized a Spanish national to extend her lease upon its expiration.[97] In the following several years the Commission Supérieure de Cassation applied its new doctrine to Swiss, British and Italian nationals and it was evident that it would do so in all cases described in the circular.[98]

This would probably have been the end of the story, except that after 1926 the cases involving commercial leases no longer went to the Commission Supérieure de Cassation. Prior to 1920 all rent control cases had gone through the normal appeal channels to the Civil Chamber of the Cour de Cassation. However, by 1920 the Civil Chamber had become so overburdened that the Commission Supérieure de Cassation was created to consider only rent control cases.[99] It had the status of a chamber of the Cour de Cassation but its membership was drawn from both the Cour de Cassation and the Court of Appeal of Paris, and it operated on an accelerated procedure which bypassed the court of appeal. It was this tribunal which had so quickly succumbed to the circular of the Minister of Foreign Affairs. Following the enactment of the law of June 30, 1926 on commercial leases, a statute which was not considered to be a rent control law, appeals in commercial lease cases no longer went to the Commission Supérieure de Cassation. Instead, they went through the regular courts of appeal to the Civil Chamber of the Cour de Cassation just as they had prior to 1920.

It was 1931 before the first case under the law of June 30, 1926 was decided

[97] Landelle v. Cavaillero, Comm. sup. cass., Nov. 21, 1929, D.P. 1932. 1. 113 (2e espèce) (note Devaux), S. 1930. 2. 161 (note Audinet).

[98] Blanc v. Codaghengo, Comm. sup. cass., Nov. 28, 1929, D.P. 1932. 1. 113 (3e espèce, Swiss); Burnup v. Dolphens, Comm. sup. cass., Jan. 2, 1930, *ibid.* (5e espèce, British), Amadori v. Gingot, Comm. sup. cass., June 26, 1930, *ibid.* (7e espèce, Italian).

[99] Law of Dec. 14, 1920, J.O. Dec. 16, 1920, D.P. 1921. 4. 230. From the enactment of the law of March 9, 1918 until May 31, 1920 there were 1,036,388 rent control cases filed with the arbitral commissions, the court of first instance. As of May 31, 1920, 450,815 cases had been settled, 144,466 cases had been abandoned, 173,935 decisions had been rendered and 267,172 cases remained on the docket. In addition, from October 18, 1918 to December 14, 1920, the date on which the Commission Supérieure de Cassation came into existence, the Civil Chamber of the Cour de Cassation delivered 10,447 decisions. Tournier, note to the law of March 31, 1922, D.P. 1922. 4. 73.

by the Civil Chamber.[100] The decision had been long awaited. Although the Commission Supérieure de Cassation had acceeded to the right of the Minister of Foreign Affairs to give a binding interpretation of the treaties, eleven decisions coming from six different courts of appeal had denied the right of a foreigner to extend his lease, decisions rendered both before and after the letter from the Minister of Foreign Affairs. Petitions for *cassation* had been filed in ten of those cases on behalf of the foreign lessee. The authors were split both on the question of the authority of the Minister of Foreign Affairs to interpret the treaty and on the proper interpretation.[101]

The Civil Chamber upheld the decision below that a Spanish national could not extend a commercial lease against his landlord's wishes. It interpreted article 19 of the law of June 30, 1926, in the light of its legislative history to say that a new right had been created under civil law for the sole benefit of French nationals. The statute was not intended to benefit even those foreigners whose country was linked to France by a treaty of establishment except under the conditions of article 11 of the Civil Code, namely that there was in existence in their country analogous legislation from which French nationals could benefit.

It might have been better for the Civil Chamber if it had rested at this point. It had interpreted the statute in a manner clearly consistent with the legislative will as expressed both in the wording of the statute and in the legislative history.

However, the Civil Chamber went on to interpret the 1862 treaty with Spain, the treaty which was at issue in the case. It asserted the right to do so since the conflict was of private interests. Procureur Général Matter had informed the court that in litigation concerning private interests the courts had had the sole authority to interpret treaties at least since the *Duke of Richmond*,[102] absent, of course, a new treaty which interpreted the earlier treaty. He had been less sure of the result where the two countries had exchanged simple notes or letters, but he was clear that the Minister of Foreign Affairs could not unilaterally interpret a treaty so as to bind the courts as he purported to have done in respect to the treaty with Spain in the circular of July 22, 1929.

The Civil Chamber interpreted the 1862 treaty with Spain in the light of the traditional learning which had developed around article 11 of the Civil

[100] Sanchez v. Gozland, Cass. civ., Dec. 22, 1931, D.P. 1932. 1. 131 (concl. Matter, note note Trasbot), S. 1932. 1. 257 (concl. Matter, note Niboyet).

[101] On all these matters see the thorough discussion in the conclusions of the Procureur Général Matter.

[102] Napier v. Lennox, Duke of Richmond, Cass. civ., June 24, 1839, S. 1839. 1. 577, Jour. Pal. 1839. 2. 208.

Code. To the extent that a legal right was not a product of the *jus gentium*, and the right to extend a lease after its expiration was certainly not such a right, it could be exercised by Spaniards in France only to the extent that French citizens could exercise the same right in Spain. Since there was no Spanish legislation which provided for the extension of an expired commercial lease, the Spanish plaintiff could not claim such a right in France.[103]

The Commission Supérieure de Cassation immediately followed the lead of the Civil Chamber by holding that the treaty with Chile, which the Minister of Foreign Affairs had said in the 1929 circular contained a clause assimilating Chilean nationals to French nationals, granted to Chilean nationals only the right to be treated in France in the same manner that French subjects are treated in Chile.[104] However, the Commission Supérieure de Cassation also held that the exchange of letters between the French and Swiss governments interpreting the Franco-Swiss treaty amounted to a bilateral interpretation of the treaty which was binding on the courts.[105]

The Minister of Foreign Affairs immediately saw the way out of his difficulty. He exchanged letters with Belgium, Panama, Spain and the United States and had these letters and the previous letters with the British and Swiss governments published in the Official Journal by presidential decrees.[106]

When the problem next returned to the Civil Chamber after the publication of the presidential decrees it involved the Swiss treaty and the letters of interpretation.[107] Not unexpectedly the Civil Chamber conformed to the interpretation given by the Minister of Foreign Affairs. With no continuing support from the Parliament in support of its legislative intent to exclude foreigners with or without a treaty, it was difficult for the court to withstand the continuing pressure from the Minister of Foreign Affairs supported by the President.

The Civil Chamber acknowledged that the exchange of letters of 11-26 July 1929 with the Swiss government published by a presidential decree

[103] One of the poignant aspects of the case was that the plaintiff became a French citizen before the expiration of his lease, though after the date on which it had been necessary for him to inform his landlord of his intent to extend the lease. The Civil Chamber held that the effective date for measuring his rights was the date of notification.

[104] Schreiber v. Ragaru, Comm. sup. cass., Dec. 1, 1932, D.H. 1933. 7.

[105] Huckendubler v. Hoeffleur, Comm. sup. cass., Dec. 22, 1932, D.H. 1933. 39.

[106] Belgium, decree of June 30, 1934, J.O. July 10, 1934, D.P. 1935. 4. 27; Great Britain, decree of June 16, 1933, J.O. June 18, 1933, D.P. 1933. 4. 238; Panama, decree of Nov. 18, 1933, J.O. Nov. 21, 1933, D.P. 1934. 4. 36; Spain, decree of April 16, 1933, J.O. April 21, 1933, D.P. 1933. 4. 154; Switzerland, decree of June 16, 1933, J.O. June 18, 1933. D.P. 1933. 4. 238; United States, decree of May 9, 1933, J.O. May 13, 1933, D.P. 1933. 4. 156. The benefits of the lease legislation had also been specifically extended to Greek citizens by *addendum* arts. 19 and 20 of the treaty of March 11. 1929, J.O. October 22, 1929, B.L.D. 1929. 431.

[107] Zumkeller v. Florence, Cass. civ., Feb. 4, 1936, D.H. 1936. 145, S. 1936. 1. 257 (note Raynaud).

constituted a diplomatic accord which interpreted and became a part of the 1882 treaty. This was not in and of itself enough for the treaty to prevail. If the letters simply indicated the intention of the drafters in 1882, the treaty rule dated from 1882 and the statute, which was later in time, had to prevail unless the treaty somehow prevented the Parliament from enacting an inconsistent statute. On the other hand if the letters were to be taken as a new international agreement subsequent to the conflicting statutes, there was the constitutional question whether they could become self-executing in France absent parliamentary approval. The Civil Chamber avoided the two horns of the dilemma by interpreting the statute of June 30, 1926 as "necessarily" excluding the case where a foreigner could invoke a treaty.

Although the precedential effect of the decision could have been limited to only those countries with which letters of interpretation had been exchanged, the Cour de Cassation recognized that the citizens of all countries listed in the 1929 circular or which later negotiated a treaty with France containing an assimilation or most-favored-nation clause were to receive the benefits of the lease statutes.[108] The court was not about to require a formality with which the other states would have been only too happy to comply.

Some of the lower courts continued to resist the application of the two 1926 statutes to foreigners who claimed the benefit of a treaty. This resistance increased when the 1926 statutes were replaced on the outbreak of World War II by new rent control legislation more closely geared to the wartime needs. Again, the legislation was specifically restricted to French subjects, residents of the protectorates and those who served in the French or allied armies or whose descendants served in such armies subsequent to September 1, 1939.[109] It was not long before the foreign governments again complained to the French Government.

The response was in the form of the law of May 28, 1943.[110] It stated that it was an interpretative statute, affecting all ordinary or extraordinary statutes governing leases of dwellings or of farms. It went on to say that notwithstanding any restrictive provisions, those statutes were "necessarily" applicable to foreign nationals from states which offered an analogous legislation to French citizens, which thereby made the provisions of article 11 of the Civil Code a formal part of all lease statutes. The law of May 28, 1943 also said that the benefits of the lease statutes were available to those foreign nationals who were exempted from such reciprocity by treaty. The law continued in article 2 by saying that the treaties envisaged by article 1 were those

[108] Simon-Depitre, L'activité professionnelle des étrangers en France 83 (1955).
[109] Decree-law of Sept. 26, 1939, art. 25, J.O. 1939. 12024, D.P. 1939. 4. 476.
[110] Law No. 289 of May 28, 1943, J.O. 1943. 2046, D.A. 1943. L. 113.

which directly or indirectly assimilated the foreigners in question to a French national in respect to *droits civils* or at least in respect to those *droits civils* relevant to the statute whose benefits the foreigner had claimed.

The statute was very awkward, obviously through an attempt to capitalize on the prior history of the controversy.[111] Nevertheless, it accomplished its task. As a law there was little doubt of its binding character on the courts. Nor was there any serious question but that the legislator intended the nationals of at least the 31 states mentioned in the 1929 circular to benefit from the provisions of all legislation governing leases then in effect. And there has been no question of its continuing validity even though it was originally enacted by the Vichy regime.

The most important problem which arose after 1943 was the application of the law to the comprehensive law governing farm leases enacted in 1945.[112] A 1946 amendment restricted its benefits to a limited number of foreigners.[113] There was some question whether either the 1943 law of interpretation or the ministerial interpretation of the treaties limited the restrictive effect of this statute. In the end the Cour de Cassation again recognized that most foreigners who could rely upon a treaty could exercise the rights created by the statute.[114]

The controversy as to whether the benefits of the various lease statutes could be denied to those foreigners who could rely upon a treaty had been active for thirty years. It ended in the effective superiority of the treaties which contained assimilation or most-favored-nation clauses over the legislation concerning various forms of leases in which the Parliament had consistently attempted to deny the access of most foreigners to certain important benefits. Professor Niboyet had hailed as "an important step towards the respect for treaties"[115] the 1936 decision by which the Civil Chamber had given the benefits of the commercial lease statute to a Swiss national on the basis of the Government's interpretation of the Swiss treaty of 1882 and a second decision rendered the following day by a different chamber of the

[111] Basdevant, Commentaire, D.C. 1944. L. 34.

[112] Ordonnance No. 45-2380 of Oct. 17, 1945, J.O. 1945. 6614, D. 1944. L. 25.

[113] Art. 61 of ordonnance No. 45-2380 of Oct. 17, 1945 (now C. Rural, art. 869), added by law No. 46-682 of April 13, 1946, art. 21, J.O. 1946. 3131, D. 1946. L. 171.

[114] Verbriggne v. Bellest, Cass. soc., July 11, 1947, D. 1947. Jur. 396, S. 1947. 1. 198, J.C.P. 1947. II. 3950 (note Ourliac et de Juglart) (Belgium). The benefits of the farm lease law were denied to Spaniards in Marco v. Fabresse, Cass. civ. soc., Nov. 25, 1948, D. 1949. Jur. 27 (1re espèce), J.C.P. 1949. II. 4650 (note Ourliac et de Juglart), 38 Rev. Crit. D.I.P. 306 (note Monneray) (1949). For the current status of the rights of foreigners under the farm lease law see Simon-Depitre, *La condition des étrangers en France*, Juris-Classeur, Droit International fasc. 525-C, ¶¶ 86-121 (1960 with *mise à jour*); Ourliac et de Juglart, *La condition des fermiers et des métayers étrangers*, J.C.P. 1969. I. 2228.

[115] Niboyet, *Un pas appréciable vers le respect des traités*, D.H. 1936. chron. 41.

Cour de Cassation in which a petition for *excès de pouvoir* brought by the Procureur Général had been used to annul a decision by a lower court which had not applied a pertinent treaty.[116] Professor Niboyet might better have called these decisions an important step towards the Government's control of the interpretation of treaties in the courts.

The battle over the lease legislation was fought in isolation. Throughout the 1920s when the Ministry of Foreign Affairs became committed to protecting the rights of foreigners to the benefits of the two statutes there were few other acts of discrimination against foreigners. However, by 1936 when the Ministry won the decisive battle about which Professor Niboyet was so pleased, the French promises to assimilate foreigners to the legal rights of French citizens had begun to crumble before the beggar-thy-neighbor economic policies practiced by all Western states during the economic depression. By the late 1940s and early 1950s when the last acts in the lease controversy were drawing to a close with the affirmance of the applicability of most of the assimilation and most-favored-nation clauses to farm leases, the Ministry of Foreign Affairs was ready to use its authority to impose its interpretation of treaties on the courts as a means of protecting the right of France to discriminate against foreigners.

CARTE DE COMMERÇANT 1950 TO 1960

The discrimination in question was the necessity for foreigners to secure a permit called a *carte de commerçant* before they could engage in business activities. Comparable work permits and permits to operate a farm are also required, though neither has figured significantly in the litigation.[117] No permit to engage in a non-salaried activity had been required prior to the late 1930s.[118] It had been accepted doctrine that commerce was to be free of governmental interference, and this had included the freedom for foreigners to engage in business in France. Only a few of the established professions such as law and medicine and a sprinkling of business activities were closed to them.

[116] Pick v. Bernheim, Cass. req., Feb. 5, 1936, S. 1936. 1. 151.

[117] See Rodriguez v. Gassion, Cass. civ. 3e, May 16, 1972, J.C.P. 1972. II. 17224 (note Ourliac et de Juglart); Roques v. Van der Swallen, Cass. soc., Feb. 6, 1959, D. 1959. somm. 62, 50 Rev. Cr. D.I.P. 524 (note Simon-Depitre) (1961), on *renvoi* Cour d'appel de Nimes, March 10, 1966, D.S. 1966, somm. 122, 56 Rev. Cr. D.I.P. 307 (note Simon-Depitre) (1967); Min. de l'Agriculture v. Michels, Conseil d'État, Oct. 4, 1967, 24 Act. Jur. Dr. Ad. 169 (concl. Braibant) (1968), 95 Clunet 733 (obs. B.G.) (1968).

[118] Work permits for salaried activities were first required by the law of Aug. 11, 1926, J.O. 1, 21926, D.P. 1927. 4. 172.

By the late 1930s the previous pride in the large number of foreigners resident in France had given way to a general desire for a France for Frenchmen. This was due to a number of factors among which the economic depression and the great influx of foreigners ranked high.[119]

France, like most other Western states, attempted to increase the already large protection which her economy enjoyed from foreign influences, whether those foreign influences were located abroad or at home.[120] Higher tariffs, quotas, and exchange controls were major tools in the attempted construction of a self-sufficient economy. On the domestic scene foreign firms were limited in the extent to which they could establish manufacturing and distribution facilities inside France. One method by which this was accomplished was to prohibit foreigners from entering a specific industry, or, where penetration had already occurred, to restrict all new enterprises from being established.[121] Another method of attack was to limit the general right of foreigners to engage in business.

A decree of June 17, 1938, limited the commercial activities of foreigners to those activities in which their country permitted French citizens to engage. In addition, the decree provided that the number of foreigners in any given economic activity was to be limited by decrees to be issued in the future.[122] The decree of June 17, 1938 was never implemented. It was supplemented by a new decree of November 12, 1938, which required all foreigners engaged in industry and commerce [artisanal activities were added by a later decree] to secure a special identity card.[123] Although foreigners were permited to engage only in the specific activity listed on their card, amendment was easily accomplished. There was in fact no control over the commercial or professional activities of foreigners admitted to residence. Once the Ministry of the Interior had granted the right of residence, the right to work was taken for granted.

With the close of World War II steps were taken to liberalize the French society. Among them was the ordonnance of November 2, 1945 which eased

[119] The number of foreigners resident in France had gone from 1,132,696 in 1911 to 2,891,168 in 1931. Extract from the Census of 1954 reproduced in Simon-Depitre, L'activité professionnelle des étrangers en France 376 (1955).

[120] "The autarchic movement of these recent years is at its base essentially for professional protection. It tends to protect manual or intellectual work, as the case may be, against foreign competition, [interests which are] always professional." Josserand, *La renaissance des droits "civils,"* D.H. 1937. chron. 69, 72.

[121] E.g., law "tending to protect the industry and retail distribution of shoes," March 22, 1936, J.O. March 23-24, 1936, D.P. 1936, 4. 155. See especially the note to the law in Dalloz by Michel Debré, then a young member of the Conseil d'État.

[122] J.O. June 26, 1938, D.P. 1938. 4. 337.

[123] J.O. Nov. 12-13, 1938, D.P. 1939. 4. 166.

the conditions for the entry and the residence of foreigners.[124] Although the ordonnance required work permits for salaried employees, it did not of itself require any permit for non-salaried professionals. It merely said they"could" be required to receive an authorization to engage in specified activities. In accordance with standard French practice the ordonnance contained a blanket repealer clause of "all dispositions contrary to the present ordonnance." There followed a long debate whether the mandatory requirement of a *carte de commerçant* found in the decree of November 12, 1938 had been repealed, but the Cour de Cassation in 1948 and the Conseil d'État in 1951 held that it was still in force.[125]

Until the ordonnance of November 2, 1945, the identity card issued to foreigners served both as a residence permit and as a work permit or *carte de commerçant*. Following the adoption of the ordonnance and as their identity cards expired the foreigners were required to procure a separate identity card from the Ministry of the Interior, which is charged with the entry and residence of foreigners, and a work peımit from the Ministry of Labor or a *carte de commerçant* from the Ministry of Commerce.

No real problems had arisen over the application of the 1938 decree until after the ordonnance of November 2, 1945, separated the identity card from the *carte de commerçant*. In large measure this was because all business activities had been subject to strict and sometimes arbitrary controls from the beginning of the war in 1939 until 1945. If any differential treatment of foreigners existed, it had been effectively screened from view. However, soon after the introduction of the separate *carte de commerçant* and its control by the Ministry of Commerce some foreign merchants whose identity cards had expired had difficulties in securing a *carte de commerçant*. Criminal proceedings were begun against those foreign merchants who continued to engage in business without one.

The lower court decisions went in three separate directions. There were some which applied the decree, others which applied the treaties, and a few which attempted to reconcile the decree with France's treaty obligations.

Some of the courts which applied the decree relied upon the 1948 decision of the Cour de Cassation which, in holding that the decree had not been repealed by the ordonnance of November 2, 1945, had said, "The decree-law of November 12, 1938 ... contain[s] no exemption to the obligation resting on a foreigner who exercises a commercial, industrial or artisanal profession

[124] Ordonnance No. 45-2658 of Nov. 2, 1945, J.O. 1945. 7225, D. 1946. L. 24.

[125] Scanu, Cass. crim., Dec. 30, 1948, D. 1949. Jur. 84, 38 Rev. Cr. D.I.P. 311 (1949); Galetzky, Conseil d'État, June 15, 1951, D. 1951. Jur. 531, S. 1951. 3. 93 (note M.L.), 41 Rev. Cr. D.I.P. 85 (note Loussouarn) (1952).

to be the holder of a special identity card bearing the commercial designation."[126] However, the defendant in the case had claimed an exemption from the requirement on the grounds of his long residence in France. The Cour de Cassation had not been called upon to apply a treaty and that question remained unresolved.

A more important reason advanced for applying the decree was the same as that which had been advanced for excluding foreigners from the benefits of the lease legislation. The decree was said to be a exercise of the police power regulating the control of foreigners. As a result it could be said that the decree would displace any prior treaty provision[127] or, alternatively, that the treaty did not intend to limit France's sovereign power to institute a general control of all foreigners by requiring passports, visas, residence permits or *cartes de commerçant*.[128] The Franco-Spanish treaty, it was said, is intended only to determine the rights of a Spaniard under the *droit civil*, and not to guarantee them against the exercise of the police power.

In one decision the Court of Appeal of Paris attempted to reconcile the obligation to have a *carte de commerçant* with the assimilation clause in the Franco-Spanish treaty by holding that possession of the card was necessary but that the Government was required to issue one to any Spanish citizen upon request.[129] The difficulty with this argument was that the Court of Appeal of Paris had no comptence to require the Government to issue a *carte de commerçant* and neither the Government nor the Conseil d'État agreed that Spaniards had an automatic right to have one issued to them.

The vast majority of the early court decisions took the position that the decree of November 12, 1938 was not applicable where the foreigner was the beneficiary of either an assimilation or a most-favored-nation clause in a treaty. This seemed the obvious conclusion to be drawn from the entire history of the lease legislation. Moreover, the principle of the supremacy of treaties over domestic law had been posed for the first time in French constitutional law in articles 25 and 28 of the Constitution of 1946. There was every reason to believe that the Criminal Chamber would confirm the applicability of the treaties when it had the opportunity.

On March 24, 1953, the Criminal Chamber gave its long awaited decision in three cases decided in practically identical words. Two decisions quashed

[126] Scanu, Cass. crim., Dec. 30, 1948, D. 1949. Jur. 84, 38 Rev. Cr. D.I.P. 311 (1949).

[127] Coll, Cour d'appel de Paris, Jan. 29, 1951, Gaz. Pal. 1952. I. 366, 41 Rev. Cr. D.I.P. 469 (1re espèce) (note Freyria) (1952).

[128] Madrid, Tribunal correctionnel de la Seine, March 11, 1953, Gaz. Pal. 1953. I. 248.

[129] Coll, Cour d'appel de Paris, Jan. 24, 1952, J.C.P. 1952. II. 7056, 41 Rev. Cr. D.I.P. 469 (note Freyria) (1952).

acquitals of Spaniards[130] and one quashed the conviction of an Italian[131] on the ground that the courts of appeal should have requested the interpretation of the treaty in question by the Minister of Foreign Affairs.

In accordance with the standard procedure in the Cour de Cassation the Criminal Chamber did not itself pose the questions to the Minister of Foreign Affairs. The error in the courts of appeal was not the substantive error in the interpretation given to the treaty, it was the procedural error of failing to request an interpretation from the Minister. The cases were, therefore, remanded to new courts of appeal with an indication that the appropriate questions were (1) whether the treaties in question authorized a Spanish or Italian subject to engage in commerce in France without a *carte de commerçant*, and (2) whether on a reciprocal basis French subjects were free to direct a commercial enterprise in Spain or Italy without prior authorization.

It was not exactly clear what the Criminal Chamber had in mind when it suggested the second of these two questions. It may have felt that even if the treaty did not authorize Spaniards or Italians to engage in commerce without a *carte de commerçant*, they would be authorized to do so on a reciprocal basis if French subjects were allowed to do so in Spain or Italy. Perhaps the Criminal Chamber thought that legislative reciprocity was an additional requirement in the tradition of article 11 of the Civil Code.[132]

The lower courts did the bidding of the Criminal Chamber and posed the suggested questions to the Minister of Foreign Affairs. The responses, signed by the Director of Administrative and Social Affairs of the Ministry of Foreign Affairs and sent directly to the requesting courts, uniformly interpreted the Spanish and Italian treaties not to relieve Spanish and Italian citizens from the "measures of control which the state of residence considers necessary to take in regard to foreigners for reasons of public order."[133]

Even though the responses were clear, the courts were not in agreement over their obligation. The Conseil d'État and some of the courts applied the interpretation as they received it.[134] On the other hand the Court of Appeal of

[130] Ara-Arroyos, Cass. crim., March 24, 1953, J.C.P. 1953. II. 7659 (note Weil et Leauté), 42 Rev. Cr. D.I.P. 573 (note Brouchot) (1953), 80 Clunet 645 (note Goldman); Sanchez, Cass. crim., March 24, 1953, D. 1953. Jur. 365 (note Savatier).

[131] Bruni, Cass. crim., March 24, 1953, D. 1953. Jur. 425. *Bruni* was also reported as a companion case to *Ara-Arroyos* in the three journals cited above.

[132] Simon-Depitre, L'activité professionnelle des étrangers en France 43-47 (1955), and notes to the decisions of March 24, 1953, *supra*.

[133] Quoted in Min. public v. G..., Tribunal correctionnel de la Seine, Dec. 4, 1954, 43 Rev. Cr. D.I.P. 778 (1954).

[134] Bertrina, Conseil d'État, March 18, 1955, 45 Rev. Cr. D.I.P. 48 (2e espèce) (note Simon-Depitre) (1956); Jiminez, Cour d'appel de Toulouse, May 24, 1954, D. 1954. Jur. 446, Gaz. Pal. 1954. 2. 69; Bruni, Cour d'appel de Limoges, Nov. 19, 1953, D. 1954. somm. 46, Gaz. Pal. 1954. 1. 258.

Paris held that it was not bound by a unilateral interpretation contained in a letter which was neither signed by the Minister nor published in the Official Journal.[135] It then went on to interpret the treaty as precluding the application of the decree, and held that the superiority of treaties over domestic law called for a dismissal of the prosecution.

When the Criminal Chamber received a petition for *cassation* by the Government from a decision which had dismissed the prosecution of a Spaniard, it agreed with the Court of Appeal of Paris that the courts were not bound by an interpretation rendered by the Government in such an informal manner.[136] However, it disagreed with the conclusion that the prosecution should have been dismissed. It said that the questions should have been posed again to the Minister of Foreign Affairs, this time indicating the form of response which was necessary.

The questions were posed again by the lower courts and the Minister of Foreign Affairs himself signed the letter to the Minister of Justice dated April 15, 1957. The Minister of Justice in turn distributed the letter by a circular published in the Official Journal.[137]

It was no surprise that the Minister's letter firmly stated that "Spanish subjects cannot invoke the convention of January 7, 1862, to remove themselves from the obligation of being holders of the special card which all foreign merchants must own." Nevertheless, the letter gave lip service to the principles for which the Ministry of Foreign Affairs had fought so hard during the long debate over the lease legislation. The Spanish treaty was a treaty which assimilated Spanish subjects to the rights of French subjects. Therefore, it was of no interest to inquire into the rights of French subjects in Spain as did the second question suggested by the Criminal Chamber. There was no expectation that the rights of Spanish subjects in France and French subjects in Spain would be equal. Such a treaty would be a treaty of reciprocity, not a treaty of assimilation. If Spain failed to abide by her treaty obligations, the French Government and not the courts would take the appropriate action. The French courts need assure themselves only that Spanish subjects received national treatment in the exercise of their rights in France.

However, the requirement of procuring a *carte de commerçant* did not affect the exercise of the right to engage in commerce, but merely the conditions under which the right could be exercised. The foreigner "must be able

[135] Vallès, Cour d'appel de Paris, April 1, 1954, D. 1954. Jur. 280; Hurtado, Cour d'appel de Paris, April 1, 1954, Gaz. Pal. 1954. 1. 337; Sastella, Cour d'appel de Paris, April 1, 1954, *ibid.*

[136] Hurtado, Cass. crim., March 10, 1955, 45 Rev. Cr. D.I.P. 48 (note Simon-Depitre) (1956).

[137] Circular of May 15, 1957, J.O. 1957. 5235, D. 1957. L. 185.

to prove that [notwithstanding the fact that he is a foreigner] he can claim the privileges of a Frenchman in the exercise of a particular right." Therefore, said the Minister's letter, "the possession of a *carte de commerçant* as regards the foreigner assimilated to the national is a necessary condition at the same time as a sufficient one to admit him to the regime applicable to nationals."

Suprisingly enough, several courts of appeal continued to resist the application of the decree. The Court of Appeal of Poitiers said that the Minister's letter did not interpret the treaty, which was moreover "perfectly clear," but instead interpreted the decree of November 12, 1938. The Minister's interpretation of the decree was "not binding on the courts which alone are competent to say if the application of a legislative text of internal law is or is not compatible with the dispositions of an unambiguous international convention."[138]

The Court of Appeal of Colmar attacked the Minister's interpretation head on. It said that the claimed distinction "between the possession of a right to engage in commerce which is free and the exercise of its right which is not free is a subtlety which leads to the impairment of a right solemnly guaranteed by a convention to which France engaged its signature.... One cannot speak of the possession of a right if the one who is recognized as having the possession is not permitted to exercise it."[139] The court went on to say that treaties must be executed in good faith. If the circumstances render a treaty dangerous for the national economy, it is up to the Government to denounce it in order to replace it with one which is less liberal. In the meantime, this role cannot be taken on by the courts which must assure the scrupulous application of the treaties.

As late as 1962 the Criminal Court of the Seine calmly cited article 55 of the 1958 Constitution, the most-favored-nation clause in the Italian treaty and the assimilation clause in the Spanish treaty as the basis for its acquital of an Italian for engaging in commerce without a card.[140]

As might have been expected the Criminal Chamber supported the Minister in every case to come its way and it appears that the revolt among the lower courts is over.[141] All foreigners need a *carte de commerçant* to engage in business activities, an agriculture card to operate a farm or a work permit to take a salaried job, unless they are exempted by the decree itself.

[138] Min. public v. Miguel, Cour d'appel de Poitiers, Dec. 20, 1957, 48 Rev. Cr. D.I.P. 88 (note Simon-Depitre) (1959).

[139] Pellacia, Cour d'appel de Colmar, Nov. 7, 1958, *ibid.*

[140] Min. public v. Sciama, Tribunal correctionnel de la Seine, Nov. 27, 1962, 52 Rev. Cr. D.I.P. 270 (1963), Gaz. Pal. 1963. 1. 199.

[141] The most recent decision is Aschbacher, Cass. crim. Jan. 22, 1963, D. 1963. Jur. 531, S. 1964. Jur. 41.

That appears to be the end of the story in respect to the *carte de commerçant* in the criminal courts. However, following the suggestion of the Court of Appeal of Paris some foreigners to whom cards were refused sought relief from the administrative tribunals. The Conseil d'État has generally denied any relief. It has ruled that the Government is not limited to the reasons outlined in the decree for rejecting an application for a *carte de commerçant* but may exercise its discretion.[142] The only limits on the exercise of administrative discretion are that the reasons for rejection must relate to factors peculiar to the applicant rather than be of a general nature[143] and they may not be based on an incorrect assessment of the law.[144] As a practical matter these two limitations have little effect on the administration.

The dispute over the *carte de commerçant* not only limited the value of the right of establishment clauses in the existing treaties, it also affected the language of such clauses in the new treaties. Until about 1950 the Ministry of Foreign Affairs had continued to include assimilation and most-favored-nation clauses without qualification.[145] In the treaties negotiated after 1950 both parties reserved the right "to take measures that are necessary for the maintenance of public order and for the protection of public health, morals and safety."[146] As a result these new treaties negotiated with such countries as Germany and the United States no longer purport to protect their citizens against legislation which reserves benefits under a statute to French citizens or which requires a permit to engage in economic activities.

A countervailing trend also began in 1950 when France proposed the first of the European Communities, the European Coal and Steel Community. One of the more important accomplishments of the Communities to date has been the gradual elimination of restrictions on the right of establishment of Community nationals in other Member States. The effect in France has been to eliminate the requirement of a *carte de commerçant* for Community nationals to engage in the activities which have been liberated by a Com-

[142] Galetzky, Conseil d'État, June 15, 1951, D. 1951. Jur. 531, S. 1951. 3. 93 (note M.L.).

[143] *Ibid.* The reason given by the Minister of Industry and Commerce for refusing to issue a *carte de commerçant* was that "all available shops are in principle reserved for French citizens." In Min. de l'Agriculture v. Michels, Conseil d'État, Oct. 4, 1967, 24 Act. Jur. Dr. Ad. 169 (concl. Braibant) (1968), 95 Clunet 733 (observ. B.G.) (1968), the Conseil d'État held that the Minister of Agriculture was authorized to refuse a permit to operate a farm on the grounds that the Department of the Somme had more farmers than there were farms available.

[144] Secrétaire d'État au commerce intérieur v. Hurni, Conseil d'État, April 7, 1965, J.C.P. 1965. II. 14172 bis, 54 Rev. Cr. D.I.P. 532 (1965). Since a Swiss citizen has the right under the treaty of establishment to hold a liquor license, a *carte de commerçant* cannot be denied on the grounds that it is intended to be used to open a cafe.

[145] Piot, *Of Realism in Conventions of Establishment*, 88 Clunet 39 (1961).

[146] Convention of Establishment between the United States of America and France, Nov. 25, 1959, art. II., para. 3, 11 U.S.T. 2398, T.I.A.S. No. 4625, ratified in France by decree No. 60-1330 of Dec. 7, 1960, J.O. 1960. 11220, D. 1961. L. 3.

munity directive.[147] The laws in regard to commercial and farm leases have also been modified to accord Community nationals the same rights as French citizens, but again only to the extent that the commercial activity has been liberated.[148] While this latter change in the law was of no importance to the citizens of Belgium and Luxembourg, to whom these rights were already available under their treaties of establishment, it extended the preemptive right to purchase farm land they were working to Dutch and Italian share-croppers, who did not have this right under their particular treaties. As to German lessees, their pre-war treaty lapsed on account of World War II and article IV (1) of the treaty of October 27, 1956 contains one of the new style clauses which granted them no rights in fact.[149] Therefore, the new modification of the law brings them in line with the rights possessed by other Community nationals, except that Germans still have no right to extend a commercial lease for a commercial activity not yet liberated, they have no right to extend a lease on their dwelling, and German landlords have no right to repossess property for their personal, family or commercial use on the termination of a lease. These rights may, of course, yet be granted to German nationals by future extensions of the right of establishment under Community law.[150]

THE REACTION 1960 TO 1970

Interpretation

The confrontation over the lease legislation and the subsequent history of the *carte de commerçant* demonstrated that the most important question in respect to the legal effect of a treaty in the French courts is whether it will be interpreted by the courts or by the Government. In the crucial cases the courts and the Government have had diametrically opposed views on the proper interpretation of the treaty and the means by which it and the statute should be reconciled. The decision that the Government had the authority to give a binding interpretation to the treaties in both the lease and the *carte de*

[147] Ordonnance No. 69-815 of Aug. 28, 1969, J.O. 1969. 8927, D.S. 1969. L. 335. Instead of referring to those activities liberated by Community directive, the ordonnance lists those activities in an annex. Therefore, it will be necessary to amend the annex as each new activity is liberated. For the permit to operate a farm or engage in other non-salaried activities in agriculture and forestry see decree No. 69-820 of Aug. 28, 1969, J.O. 1969. 8942, D.S. 1969. L. 337.

[148] Ordonnance No. 69-394 of April 22, 1969, J.O. 1969. 4262, D.S. 1969. L. 180 (commercial leases); ordonnance No. 69-819 of Aug. 28, 1969, art. 2, J.O. 1969. 8941, D.S. 1969, L. 336.

[149] Ratified by decree No. 59-1046 of Sept. 4, 1959, J.O. 1959. 8850, D. 1959 .L. 584.

[150] Simon-Depitre, *L'application en France des mesures communautaires en matière de liberté d'établissement*, 59 Rev. Cr. D.I.P. 227 (1970).

commerçant cases automatically determined how the treaties would be interpreted and, therefore, whether the statute would be applied as it was enacted.

The determination whether the courts could interpret a treaty has universally been considered a matter of law which arises out of the separation of powers. The courts have no discretionary authority to request an interpretation from the Government. Either they are obligated to interpret a given provision in a treaty or they are obligated to seek a Governmental interpretation.[151] Presumably, even when the courts are required to interpret a treaty, they could receive the Government's interpretation as a matter of information. If this ever occurs, it is not evident in the cases.

Although the *carte de commerçant* dispute appeared to reinforce the Government's preeminent authority to interpret treaties, the long range result may well be the exact opposite. The preservation of the 1929 interpretation of assimilation and most-favored-nation clauses for the benefit of the lease legislation coupled with the denial of that interpretation in respect to the *carte de commerçant* was too crude to be intellectually or politically respectable.

Whatever the motives of the Criminal Chamber in requiring the lower courts to request an interpretation, the interpretation which the Government eventually rendered could not be justified on any of the traditional grounds. First, in 1957 as in 1929 the Government had interpreted the statute fully as much as the treaty. Second, there had been no evident bilateral consultations with the foreign states concerned. Third, the interpretation of the treaties called for no expertise not possessed by the courts, either in respect to knowledge of the subject matter or based on access to the secret record of the negotiation of the treaties. Fourth, Governmental interpretation was not necessary in order to avoid embarassment with the foreign states. Application of the earlier interpretation given in the lease controversy would have led to acquittals, which was the result desired by most of the lower courts and assuredly by the foreign states.

The Ministry of Foreign Affairs may well have been embarrassed to give a response so obviously dictated completely by domestic political considerations. That may explain why the first letter interpreting the treaties was signed by the director of Administrative and Social Affairs of the Ministry of For-

[151] In État Français v. Caldumbide, Cass. civ. 3e, Nov. 7, 1969, J.C.P. 1970. II. 16248 (2e espèce) (note Ruzié), 60 Rev. Cr. D.I.P. 105 (2e espèce) (note H. B.[attifol]), discussed below, the court said that there was no question whether the Government's interpretation should have been applied by the court of appeal since the matter had not been raised by the appellant. Professor Battifol in his note commented that he would have thought this a matter of public order to be raised by the Cour de Cassation itself.

reign Affairs rather than by the Minister himself.[152] If this was an attempt to mute the political responsibility of the Ministry of Foreign Affairs for such an awkward interpretation, it is understandable why the Criminal Chamber would insist upon an "official" interpretation. An official interpretation apparently meant one signed by the Minister and published in the Official Journal, requirements which had not been found necessary except during the confrontation over the lease legislation.[153]

The *carte de commerçant* cases coupled with a case decided in 1950, in which for the first time the Cour de Cassation adopted the Government's interpretation of a nationality provision in a treaty,[154] appeared to have reversed the previous assumption that court interpretation was the norm and Governmental interpretation the exception. Indeed, for several years there appears to have been a rash of requests for interpretations.

The reaction was not long in coming. There is some indication that the Ministry of Foreign Affairs felt that it was being asked for its interpretation of treaties which the courts should have interpreted.[155] Some commentators suggested that absent a bilateral agreement, current negotiations, or a direct communication initiated by the Ministry, the courts should interpret any treaty which came before them.[156]

The first indication that the Cour de Cassation would respond to these criticisms was in a nationality case in 1960 in which the First Civil Chamber asserted the authority of the courts "to interpret diplomatic treaties in respect

[152] "It is not certain that the Quai d'Orsay appreciated the gift of the Criminal Chamber when it asked if the Treaty of 1862 did or did not exempt Spaniards from the *carte de commerçant.* The Criminal Chamber thought that the treaty should be redone, but was this the time to propose it? The embarrassment of the Quai d'Orsay was manifested by the turgid and obscure formulas which it used in replying. Hesitating to say openly that the agreed upon assimilation did not prevent the French legislation from imposing the *carte de commerçant,* without a doubt it would have preferred for the courts to say so themselves. The independence of the judges is a good diplomatic argument."

Battifol, *L'interprétation des traités diplomatiques par les tribunaux judiciaires,* Travaux du comité français de droit international privé, 1958-59, at 112-13 (1960).

[153] See in particular the note by Ruzié to Caldumbide v. État français, Cass. civ. 3e, Nov. 7, 1969, J.C.P. 1970. II. 16248, in which he approves of the generally liberal attitude of the courts to the method by which the Government's interpretation is communicated "so long as the authenticity of the official interpretation cannot be placed in doubt."

[154] Friedman, Cass. ch. réunies, April 27, 1950, S. 1950. 1. 165 (concl. Rey, note Niboyet), 40 Rev. Cr. D.I.P. 98 (concl. Rey, note Monneray). Accord, Wolf, Cass. civ., April 6, 1951, S. 1952. 1. 84, J.C.P. 1951. II. 6351 (note Aymond).

[155] See the excerpt from Société Teschendorff et Cie v. "Les Verges d'Alsace," Tribunal de grande instance de Saverne, Nov. 27, 1962, [1963] Ann. Fr. Dr. Int'l. 977.

[156] Battifol, *L'interprétation des traités diplomatiques par les tribunaux judiciaires,* Travaux du comité français de droit international privé, 1958-59, at 112-13 (1960); Boyer, *L'affaire des "scripts lombards" (Cass. civ. 1ere, 5 oct. 1965). Sur la compétence des tribunaux judiciaires en matière d'interprétation des traités,* J.C.P. 1966. I. 2036.

to not only the private interests of the parties, but in respect to their nationality, unless the provisions to be interpreted raise questions of international public law."[157]

The decision was striking in three respects. First, it was a reaffirmation of the courts' traditional authority in respect to nationality, a matter which had been in question following the 1950 decision. Second, the First Civil Chamber claimed that the courts have the authority to interpret treaties even though the interpretation involved more than the private interests of the parties. Third, the justification for Governmental interpretation was that it placed in question international public *law* rather than international public *order*. Although the term had been used in the past,[158] its use in this case seemed to some of the commentators to be a reassertion of the plenitude of the authority of the courts to interpret treaties subject to a superior Governmental authority only when some significant problem involving foreign relations was involved. No longer could the argument be raised that only the Government could interpret treaties having a penal, fiscal or social purpose, all of which affect the public order but not necessarily international public law.[159]

That this change in terminology did indicate a change in attitude was demonstrated in 1963 when the First Civil Chamber, for what may have been the first time in French legal history, quashed a decision of a court of appeal because the court of appeal had improperly stayed its proceedings in order to request an interpretation of a tax treaty with Belgium from the Ministry of Foreign Affairs.[160] The First Civil Chamber held that the court of appeal should have interpreted the treaty itself. Although this decision was made somewhat easier in that the courts had traditionally interpreted tax treaties,[161] it prepared the way for the Temporary Chamber for Expropriation, which has since become the Third Civil Chamber.

The question before the Third Civil Chamber was whether articles 18 and 19 of the Evian Agreement which recognized Algerian independence and article 17 of the protocol of judicial cooperation required France or Algeria to pay for particular private property which had been taken under eminent domain proceedings prior to Algerian independence. In contrast to the First Civil Chamber which had held that the lower court should have interpreted

[157] Moss v. Proc. Général, Cass. civ. 1re, March 22, 1960, J.C.P. 1961. II. 11936 (note Aymond), 49 Rev. Cr. D.I.P. 557 (note Mezger) (1960).

[158] See the catalogue of terms used by the courts at various times in 1 Rousseau, Principes généraux du droit international public ¶ 414 (1944).

[159] Malaurie, Note to Receveur-percepteur de Paris v. Chassagne, Cass. civ. 1re, March 19, 1963, D. 1963. Jur. 529.

[160] *Ibid.*, J.C.P. 1963. II. 13270 (note Ancel).

[161] Chrétien, *L'application et l'interprétation des clauses fiscales des traités internationaux par les tribunaux français*, 40 Rev. Cr. D.I.P. 41, 48-57 (1951).

the tax treaty with Belgium, in its 1966 decision the Third Civil Chamber complained only that the lower court did not give an adequate justification for its decision to request an interpretation from the Government. The lower court's statement that "an action to fix the indemnity for property taken under eminent domain concerns not only private interests, but such an action concerning property taken in Algeria in 1957 could have financial and even diplomatic consequences for the relations between the French state and the Algerian state" did not say which questions of public international law were in question. Therefore, it did not give enough information for the Third Civil Chamber to determine whether the lower court had acted properly.[162]

The case was remanded to the Court of Appeal of Montpellier which was expected either to interpret the treaties itself or to refer them to the Minister of Foreign Affairs, and in either case to give sufficiently detailed reasons to allow the Cour de Cassation to review that action. However, the court of appeal did neither. Instead it decided that it was authorized, or perhaps even required, to follow an interpretation of the treaties previously given by the Minister of Foreign Affairs in a similar case before the Conseil d'État. As a result it dismissed the action as one which should properly have gone to the Algerian courts.

This reasonable assumption turned out to be false. When the Third Civil Chamber heard the case for the second time it repeated its prior statement. The lower court must explain what question of public international law precludes the court from interpreting the treaties itself. The fact that the court of appeal has applied an official Governmental interpretation is not of itself sufficient.[163]

While the First and Third Civil Chambers have struck out on the still uncharted path of limiting the extent to which the lower courts can request an interpretation of a treaty from the Government, the other three civil chambers have stayed quietly on the sidelines. Only the Second Civil Chamber has had any cases worthy of comment and they have merely reaffirmed the general authority of the Government to interpret social security treaties.[164]

[162] Caldumbide v. État français, Cass. temp. exp., June 9, 1966, J.C.P. 1966. II. 14814 (note Tricaud), 57 Rev. Cr. D.I.P. 471 (note Battifol) (1968).

[163] Caldumbide v. État français, Cass. civ. 3e, Nov. 7, 1969, J.C.P. 1970. II. 16248 (1re espèce) (note Ruzié), 60 Rev. Cr. D.I.P. 105 (1re espèce) (note H. B.). In a companion case decided the same day, État français v. Caldumbide, Cass. civ. 3e, Nov. 7, 1969, *ibid.* (2e espèce), the Third Civil Chamber affirmed the decision of the same court of appeal rendered on the same day in which the court of appeal had applied the interpretation of the Minister of Foreign Affairs to hold that the French courts had jurisdiction over the particular facts.

[164] Caisse prim. sécur. soc. v. Klaiss, Cass. civ. 2e, March 28, 1962, D. 1963. Jur. 518 (note Ph. M.); 53 Rev. Cr. D.I.P. 83; di Piero, 85 Clunet 761 (2e espèce) (note J.-D. B.), Gaz. Pal. 1958. 1. 79.

Social security treaties require a uniformity of application by all the participating states. The mechanics for bilateral and multilateral consultations and interpretations at the administrative level are well developed so that what appears before the court as a unilateral interpretation may well be a bilateral or multilateral interpretation in fact.[165]

The Criminal Chamber stands apart today as always. Although its case law on the interpretation of treaties is generally discussed as part of the case law of the Cour de Cassation, it is legitimate to do so only from an organizational or from a historical point of view as has been done in this paper. From an analytical point of view, the attitudes of the Criminal Chamber might better be discussed with those of the Conseil d'État.

In both courts the emphasis is on the relationship between the individual and the state. In the Conseil d'État the individual is complaining of the action of the state, in the criminal courts it is the state which is complaining of the action of the individual.

The Criminal Chamber was the first of the chambers of the Cour de Cassation to employ the distinction between treaty interpretations which raise questions of only private interest and those which raise questions of public order in order to stay its proceedings and request an interpretation from the Minister of Foreign Affairs. Perhaps this distinction still has some merit for the Criminal Chamber. Certainly it is willing to interpret treaties when there are only private parties before it.[166]

Since the Criminal Chamber has developed essentially the same rule as the Conseil d'État of the normalcy of Governmental interpretation, it has also developed the same theory of the *acte clair*.[167] The theory of the *acte clair* is irrelevant to the civil chambers in respect to the interpretation of treaties. If they were to say that a treaty was an *acte clair*, it would mean no more than that the treaty does not raise a sufficient question of "public international law" to justify an interpretation by the Minister of Foreign Affairs.

The fact that the Criminal Chamber is formally a part of the Cour de Cassation has distorted the development of the law in respect to the interpretation of treaties. There has been a tendency on the part of the commentators and of the civil chambers to create a unified theory which reconciled the actions of all the chambers. For this reason the decision of the Criminal

[165] Valticos, *Les conventions internationales du travail (à propos de l'arrêt KLAISS de la 2e section civile du 28 mars 1962)*, 53 Rev. Cr. D.I.P. 41, 62-63 (1964).

[166] U.T.A., Cass. crim., Dec. 3, 1969, D.S. 1970. Jur. 81 (note Chauveau), J.C.P. 1970. II. 16353 (note de Juglart et du Pontavice). See also Costa, Conclusions in Oufkir, Cass. crim., Dec. 1, 1966, D.S. 1967. Jur. 23, 25-26.

[167] Costa, Conclusions in Oufkir, Cass. crim., Dec. 1, 1966, D.S. 1967. Jur. 23, 25.

Chamber in 1877 that it could not interpret a treaty because it raised questions of public order created a precedent for the civil chambers by which they felt bound.[168] Similarly, the decisions of the Criminal Chamber in the *carte de commerçant* cases created havoc for everyone else. However, the Criminal Chamber itself has had no illusions about its different status. A review of the most recent statement by one of its members in respect to its obligation to seek an interpretation from the Minister of Foreign Affairs reveals an almost exclusive concern for the prior decisions of the Criminal Chamber.[169]

Supremacy

Until after World War II the formal supremacy of treaty or statute had been little more of a problem for the courts than it had been for the Conseil d'État. There had been little reason for the courts to face the issue of formal supremacy. The techniques of reconciliation developed over a century and a half are well ingrained in the French judicial habits, are flexible in result, and are politically safe. So long as the courts recognize the functional supremacy of a treaty by use of the techniques of interpretation, they can stay well within their traditional role. The history of the lease legislation and the *carte de commerçant* demonstrate what an intrepid interpreter could do with these techniques.

Nevertheless, the question of formal supremacy of treaty or statute has been before the courts since the Constitution of 1875 required parliamentary approval of most treaties prior to ratification.[170] At first the question was whether a treaty could displace an earlier statute if it had not received parliamentary approval, either because the treaty had been concluded prior to 1875 or because it was among those treaties which did not require such approval. Even though this was answered in the affirmative in 1887,[171] it continued to be raised during the lease controversy by courts resisting the bilateral agreements of interpretation.[172]

Nevertheless, it can be said that as a formal matter the courts considered treaties on a par with statutes from the time of the Revolution of 1789 right up to the changes brought about by the Constitution of 1946. Articles 26 and 28 of the Constitution of 1946 provided that treaties are superior to

[168] Yter, Cass. crim., July 27, 1877, D.P. 1878. 1. 137, S. 1877. 1. 485.
[169] Costa, Conclusions in Oufkir, Cass. crim., Dec. 1, 1966, D.S. 1967. Jur. 23.
[170] Constitutional law of July 16-18, 1875, art. 8, D.P. 1875. 4. 114, S. 1871-75. L. 725.
[171] Grus v. Ricordi, Cass. req., July 25, 1887, D.P. 1888. 1. 5 (concl. Lepelletier, note Sarrut), S. 1888. 1. 17 (note Lyon-Caen).
[172] L... v. Société X..., Cour d'appel de Rennes, June 16, 1930, D.P. 1931. 2. 9 (note Chauveau).

French domestic legislation, and this provision was repeated with some modifications in article 55 of the Constitution of 1958.[173]

There is no need to repeat the problems which the courts would face in attempting to enforce the formal supremacy of treaty over statute based on the unconstitutionality of the statute under article 55. It would be just as much of a new venture for the ordinary courts as it would be for the Conseil d'État.

Nevertheless, the treaty supremacy clauses in articles 26 and 28 of the 1946 Constitution of 1946 and article 55 of the Constitution of 1958 have often been cited by the courts. Normally the citation is in a case which has applied the treaty on other grounds. One writer claims that only one decision has clearly rested on the constitutional supremacy of treaty over statute.[174] As a result of this ambivalence in the cases it is still unclear what effect, if any, article 55 will have on the future respect for the supremacy of treaties.

However, one of the effects of the increasing citation of article 55 must certainly be the creation of a new climate both in respect to the supremacy of treaties and in respect to the Constitution as the source of that supremacy. Perhaps the new trend is a result of the experience which the French courts have had with Community law.

[173] Constitution of Oct. 27, 1946, J.O. 1946. 9166, D. 1946. L. 422; Constitution of Oct. 4, 1958, J.O. 1958. 9151, D. 1958. L. 324.

[174] Francescakis, *Remarques critiques sur le rôle de la Constitution dans le conflit entre le traité et la loi interne devant les tribunaux judiciaires*, 58 Rev. Cr. D.I.P. 425, 430 (1969). The case cited is Pellacia, Cour d'appel de Colmar, Nov. 7, 1958, 48 Rev. Cr. D.I.P. 88 (note Simon-Depitre) (1959).

CHAPTER IV

THE COMMUNITY EXPERIENCE

Community law has fared as well in the French courts as one could legitimately have expected. Several early lower court decisions took a cavalier attitude and both the Criminal Chamber and the Conseil d'État have failed to refer prejudicial questions to the Court of Justice under article 177 in the cases which have involved the most substantial questions of Community law. However, by the end of 1972 various French courts had referred sixteen prejudicial questions to the Court of Justice, including two from the Cour de Cassation and one from the Conseil d'État.[1] Furthermore, in other cases in which no prejudicial question has been asked, the courts have begun to apply Community law as the applicable norm.

The early failures to refer prejudicial questions caused concern among Community circles, a concern which the subsequent use of article 177 has undoubtedly mitigated. However, the early concern was exaggerated while the present situation remains ambiguous. The French courts are groping towards the fruitful collaboration with the Court of Justice which the European Parliament has recently called for.[2]

THE LOWER COURTS

The fact that thirteen of the sixteen prejudicial questions have been posed by lower courts is indicative of the importance of those courts to the successful reception of Community law. Their routine application of Community law will probably be their greatest contribution. The majority of all cases are terminated in the lower courts without a petition to the Cour de Cassation.

[1] Appendix I contains the list of cases in which French courts have posed prejudicial questions.

[2] Resolution of the European Parliament, Oct. 8, 1969, 12 E.E.C. J.O. C 139/19 (1969).

Moreover, the Cour de Cassation cannot quash a decision based on Community law unless the decision was founded upon a gross error in the interpretation of the Community law or the Cour de Cassation refers a prejudicial question to the Court of Justice. Quashing indicates disagreement and disagreement usually means the existence of a legitimate dispute over the meaning of the Community text.

Quashing is even more difficult when the lower court has referred a prejudicial question to the Court of Justice. Once the Court of Justice has interpreted the Community text, that interpretation can be ignored only by a subsequent finding that the Community text as interpreted is not applicable to the case at hand,[3] a matter for legitimate disagreement between the court of appeal and the Cour de Cassation, or by a direct ruling that the French law in conflict must be applied. Whatever the hesitancy of either the lower courts or the Cour de Cassation to affirm the formal supremacy of Community law, they would also hesitate to affirm the formal inferiority of that law to French law.

The most important decisions yet rendered by the Court of Justice on the relationship of Community law to national law have been given in response to prejudicial questions coming from lower courts,[4] but not from French courts. Their questions have been restricted to routine problems of social security law and exclusive concession agreements. It is true, however, that in one notable case the Court of Appeal of Paris seems to have bent over backwards to affirm the supremacy of Community law where such assurances were not necessary to the decision.[5]

Community law is and will remain esoteric for most of the lower courts for some time to come. In spite of the many books and articles on Community law written in French and the publication of some of the decisions of the Court of Justice in French legal periodicals, many of the lower courts have neither the library resources nor the experience with Community law necessary to accomplish their task. This may explain some of the prejudicial questions they have asked. Rather than expend the energy necessary to under-

[3] In Société Manpower v. Caisse prim. Ass. maladie Strasbourg, Commission de première instance du contentieux de la sécurité sociale et de la mutualité sociale agricole du Bas-Rhin, April 21, 1971, J.C.P. 1972. II. 17025, 8 Rev. Tr. Dr. Eur. 479 (1972), after interpretation by the Court of Justice it was determined that the cause of action should be dismissed because of new facts not before the Court of Justice.

[4] E.g. Costa v. E.N.E.L., Cour de Justice des Communautés Européennes, July 15, 1964, 10 Rec. de la Cour 1141, [1961-1966 Transfer Binder] CCH Comm. Mkt. Rep. ¶ 8023; Walt Wilhelm v. Bundeskartellamt, Cour de Justice des Communautés Européennes, Feb. 13, 1969, 15 Rec. de la Cour 1, [1967-1970 Transfer Binder] CCH Comm. Mkt. Rep. ¶ 8056.

[5] La Technique Minière, L.T.M. v. Société Maschinenbau Ulm, Cour d'appel de Paris, July 7, 1965, J.C.P. 1966. II. 14578 (4e espèce), Gaz. Pal. 1965. 2. 90 (concl. Toubas).

stand this new and difficult area of law, they are authorized to receive a definitive answer from the Court of Justice. They do not even have to ask the question properly. They can simply forward their opinion which states their confusion and the Court of Justice will extract from the confusion the proper abstract question of Community law which should have been asked and proceed to answer that question.

THE COURTS OF LAST RESORT

In spite of the importance of the lower courts to the reception of Community law in France, it is legitimate to focus on the Cour de Cassation and the Conseil d'État. In part this is because their judgments and the reports, conclusions and notes published with those judgments are an additional and important source of information about Community law for the entire French legal profession. In larger measure this is because the two supreme tribunals will establish the climate in which the entire system will operate. If they visibly fulfill their obligations under Community law, the lower courts will tend to do so likewise. If they are hesitant about this incursion on French sovereignty, the lower courts will also be hesitant.

As is true in respect to treaties generally there are significant differences in the attitude towards Community law of the Conseil d'État and the Criminal Chamber on the one hand and the civil chambers of the Cour de Cassation on the other. The Conseil d'État and the Criminal Chamber are extremely conscious of the conflict between their obligations under Community law and those under French domestic law, whereas the civil chambers appear to apply Community law as a technical matter of no great political consequence.

The likely explanation for these differences in attitude is a variation of that seen above in respect to treaties generally. The cases which have come before the Conseil d'État and the Criminal Chamber have involved matters of political significance. However, the work of the civil chambers has been limited to the Community regulations for the coordination of social security and social assistance for migrant workers. While these regulations are important to the development of the Communities, they do not raise conflicts with important French political, economic or social policies such as those which the Conseil d'État and the Criminal Chamber have faced. Nevertheless, the social security cases are worthy of discussion if for no other reason than that these regulations have generated by far the largest number of prejudicial questions from French courts, twelve of the sixteen in total among which are the only two referred by the Cour de Cassation so far.

Social Security and the Civil Chambers

The Community social security regulations are part of a broader pattern of social security treaties which supplement the national law. These treaties fall into several different categories in Europe.[6] Those sponsored by the International Labor Organization attempt to secure a minimum degree of uniformity of substantive law. Bilateral treaties are designed to solve some of the problems caused by the migration of workers. Generally speaking they have affirmed the equality of treatment on a basis of reciprocity and have established rules which are as precise as possible for the coordination of efforts in order to overcome the divergencies between the legislation of the two states. Multilateral treaties are designed to provide the same kind of coordination between the law of the signatory states as is provided by the bilateral treaties, only for several states at once. Some multilateral treaties cover specialized industries, others cover the general regime of social security and social assistance. The Community regulations fall within this latter category.

Even prior to the existence of the European Economic Community the European Coal and Steel Community had prepared a draft treaty to resolve some of the problems which had arisen out of the migration of coal and steel workers between the Member States. The advent of the EEC in 1958 with its power to issue regulations in respect to social security caused the draft treaty to be modified and issued as EEC regulations 3 and 4.[7] These regulations have recently been replaced by regulation 1408/71 of June 14, 1971.[8]

Like the law they were coordinating, regulations 3 and 4 were extremely complex. However, they solved the bulk of the problems which arose and the social security administrators of the Member States immediately applied them as part of their governing law. The disagreements which were left for the courts were few and involved marginal questions of interpretation. This is well illustrated by the cases which have gone as far as the Cour de Cassation.

The first prejudicial question referred from the Cour de Cassation involved a M. Goffart, a French citizen who applied for old age benefits from the French social security office.[9] He had worked for 124 quarters in France,

[6] See generally Lyon-Caen, *Droit international de la sécurité sociale*, Juris-Classeur, Droit International, fascs. 575-578B (1959 with *mise à jour*); Ribettes-Tillhet et Bonnet, *Sécurité sociale*, Encyclopédie Dalloz, Droit International (1969), and bibliography cited therein.

[7] Regulation 3 of Sept. 25, 1958, 1 E.E.C. J.O. 561 (1958); Regulation 4 of Dec. 3, 1958, 1 E.E.C. J.O. 597 (1958).

[8] 14 E.E.C. J.O. L. 149 (1971).

[9] Caisse rég. séc. soc. du Nord-Est v. Goffart, Cass. civ. 2e, April 27, 1967, D.S. 1967. Jur. 541 (concl. Schmelck), 72 Rev. Gén. Dr. Int'l. Pub. 242 (1968).

which was more than sufficient from him to qualify for the largest possible benefits, and for an additional 24 quarters in Belgium, enough time to qualify for old age benefits in Belgium. Articles 27 and 28 of regulation 3 provided the method of calculating the benefits to which he was entitled. Essentially it said that if a person was entitled to benefits from two or more Member States, each applicable social security office should first figure his benefits under the national legislation taking into account all the time he had worked in all the Member States. The claimant would receive from each State the amount of the calculated benefits proportionate to the time he had worked in that State. In this case Belgium would pay Goffart 24/148 of the full Belgian benefits and France would pay 124/148 of the French benefits.

If a person for some reason did not qualify for the benefits in one of the Member States in which he had worked, article 28(f) provided that the other Member States should take the time into consideration for the purpose of determining the full benefits but should not take it into consideration for the purpose of reducing those benefits. Thus, if Goffart's 24 quarters had not been sufficient for him to qualify under Belgian law, France would calculate and pay his benefits on the basis of the 148 quarters.

Goffart's problem was slightly different. His 24 quarters qualified him for the Belgian old age benefits, but under Belgian law he could not receive those benefits if he continued to work, as he was doing. Therefore, since France had no prohibition on working, he applied for the full benefits under French law. The French office claimed that according to regulation 3 they were not required to pay more than 124/148 of the full benefits. Goffart was qualified to receive the Belgian benefits; it was only the payment which was suspended. As a result of this interpretation of regulation 3, Goffart would receive less benefits because he had worked for 24 quarters in Belgium than he would have received if he had worked only the 124 quarters in France.

The court of first instance and the Court of Appeal of Nancy accepted Goffart's argument and awarded him the full French benefits. On the subsequent petition for *cassation* by the social security office the Second Civil Chamber gained the distinction of being the first chamber of the Cour de Cassation to refer a prejudicial question to the Court of Justice when it accepted the thorough and forceful argument for so doing presented to it by Advocate General Schmelck.

It should be noted that this was the first time the Cour de Cassation had itself requested an interpretation of any treaty. The obligation to secure an interpretation from the Minister of Foreign Affairs is one which rests upon the lower courts. Failure to fulfill this obligation leads the Cour de Cassation to quash the judgment of the court of appeal and remand the case to another court of appeal, the procedure which occurred in the *carte de commerçant* cases. Under no circumstances, other than those arising out of Community law, does the Cour de Cassation itself refer a prejudicial question.

In responding to the question posed by the Second Civil Chamber the Court of Justice followed its general policy of interpreting the social security regulations in the manner most beneficial to the claimant, and therefore most beneficial to the free movement of workers between the Member States.[10] It agreed with the two lower French courts that Goffart should receive the full old age benefits from France on the basis of 148 quarters until such time as he was fully eligible to receive benefits from Belgium. This interpretation was given effect by the subsequent decision of the First Civil Chamber, the chamber to which the case had been transferred in the meantime.[11]

The second prejudicial question to come from the Cour de Cassation arose out of the application of M. Torrekens, a Belgian residing in France, for the "allocation for aged workers." This particular form of assistance is designed to provide a minimum level of benefits for those persons who do not qualify for the normal social security regimes. The benefits are restricted to French nationals, unless they are extended by treaty as had been done for Belgians by the Franco-Belgian protocole of January 17, 1948. To qualify the recipient's total revenue must not pass a certain sum and he must have had a salaried employment in France for a period of either 15 years or 25 years depending on certain circumstances.

Torrekens had not worked in France for 25 years, the period applicable to him, and the Franco-Belgian protocole does not provide for the cumulation of time worked in Belgium. He claimed the benefits on the ground that article 27 of regulation 3 required the French authorities to count as part of his 25 years the time he had worked in Belgium. The social security office contended that the cumulation provisions of article 27 of regulation 3 apply only to social security regimes based on employee contributions and the allocation for aged salaried workers was not such a regime. The trial court for social security matters ruled in favor of Torrekens.

The social security authorities appealed and suggested to the Court of Appeal of Douai that an interpretation of the regulation from the proper Community officials would be advisable. The court of appeal in a commendable, but mistaken, Community spirit said that the court of first instance was "wrong in thinking that they could without more ado, allow the aplication of

[10] Caisse rég. séc. soc. du Nord-Est v. Goffart, Cour de Justice des Communautés Européennes, Nov. 30, 1967, 13 Rec. de la Cour 413.

[11] Caisse rég. séc. soc. du Nord-Est v. Goffart, Cass. civ. 1re, March 21, 1968, Gaz. Pal. 1968. 2. 83, 4 Rev. Tr. Dr. Eur. 597 (1968).

Torrekens, since international conventions are acts of high administration which can only be interpreted by the powers between whom they were concluded. The proceedings should be stayed, and the parties referred for interpretation to the administrative committee provided for this purpose by article 43 of the regulations."[12]

Those who were knowledgeable in Community law reacted vigorously.[13] By this decision the Court of Appeal of Douai had made three grievous errors in Community law.

1. The court of first instance had not been "wrong in thinking that they could without more ado, allow the application of Torrekens." The court of appeal had completely missed the significance of paragraph 2 of article 177 of the Treaty. Lower courts have full authority to interpret every provision of Community law. The long history of the circumstances under which French courts must request an interpretation from the Minister of Foreign Affairs is not relevant to the obligations of the lower courts under Community law.

2. If the Court of Appeal of Douai felt the need of a prejudicial interpretation of the regulation, which was certainly within its prerogative under article 177(2), the question had to be referred to the Court of Justice and not to the administrative committee provided in article 43 of regulation 3. This committee is indeed charged, *inter alia*, "to resolve any question of administration or interpretation flowing from the provisions of this and subsequent regulations." However, the interpretations of the committee are intended to aid in the coordination of the activities of the social security authorities of the six Member States. The committee has no competence to give prejudicial interpretations to the courts.[14]

3. Article 177 permits only the national courts, not the parties, to refer prejudicial questions.

Torrekens petitioned the Cour de Cassation on the grounds that the court of appeal had violated article 177. The case was embarrasing for those who had claimed that Community law had no place for the theory of the *acte clair*. They had attacked the manner in which the Criminal Chamber and the Conseil d'État had already used the theory to justify deciding cases without referring prejudicial questions under article 177.[15] However, if there ever was an occasion for its use, this was it, and the Second Civil Chamber quashed

[12] Caisse rég. assurance vieillesse du Nord v. Torrekens, Cour d'appel de Douai, Oct. 8, 1963, D. 1964. Jur. 299 (note R. M. Ch.).

[13] See note *ibid.*

[14] Bestuur der Sociale Verzekeringsbank v. Van Der Vecht, Cour de Justice des Communautés Européennes, Dec. 5, 1967, 13 Rec. de la Cour 445.

[15] This was especially true of Chevallier. See in English, Chevallier, *Note on the case Soc. des Pétroles Shell-Berre*, 3 Comm. Mkt. L. R. 100 (1965).

the decision of the Court of Appeal of Douai and sent the case to the Court of Appeal of Amiens.[16]

Amiens agreed with the original trial court that article 27 of regulation 3 authorized Torrekens to cumulate the time worked in Belgium. The social security office petitioned the Cour de Cassation which found that there was a "serious" question of the meaning of article 27. It stayed its proceedings and sent a copy of its opinion to the Court of Justice without any precise question.[17]

The Court of Justice held, as was expected,[18] that regulation 3 required cumulation of the time worked in Belgium with that in France.[19] It left open the possibility that this result was precluded by the Franco-Belgian protocole of January 17, 1948 in respect to the allocation for aged workers since parts of the protocole remained in existence and they take precedence over regulation 3.[20]

At this stage of the proceedings the result was still not clear because the protocole had always been understood not to change the rule requiring 25 years service in France. However, the Social Chamber, to which the case had been transferred pending the response of the Court of Justice, ruled that since the effect of regulation 3 as interpreted by the Court of Justice gave French workers the right to apply their time worked in other Member States to qualify for the allocation for aged salaried workers, this right was also available to Torrekens.[21] One only hopes that he will live for a long time now that his right to benefits based in part on poverty has been vindicated after eight years of litigation.

The other social security cases in the Cour de Cassation illustrate no less of an awareness and willingness to abide by the Community regulations than do the two which resulted in the referral of prejudicial questions. They also show some of the many dificulties which the coordination of social security law has posed for the national administrative and judicial officials.

In *Union régionale des sociétés de secours minières du Nord v. Gosset* the Social Chamber quashed the decision of the Court of Appeal of Amiens

[16] Dir. rég. séc. soc. Lille v. Torrekens, Cass. civ. 2e, Dec. 1, 1965, D.S. 1966. Jur. 373 (note Chevallier), J.C.P. 1966. II. 14578 (1re espèce).

[17] Caisse rég. séc. soc. du Nord v. Torrekens, Cass. civ. soc., Oct. 24, 1968, 5 Rev. Tr. Dr. Eur. 138 (1969), 32 Droit Social 331 (obs. Lyon-Caen) (1969).

[18] See the observations by Lyon-Caen in note 17 *supra*.

[19] Caisse rég. séc. soc. du Nord v. Torrekens, Cour de Justice des Communautés Européennes, May 7, 1969, 15 Rec. de la Cour 125.

[20] Compare annexe D of regulation 3 with annexe II. A. 2. of regulation 1408/71 of June 14, 1971, 14 E.E.C. J.O. L 149/37.

[21] Caisse rég. séc. soc. du Nord v. Torrekens, Cass. civ. soc., Feb. 12, 1970, J.C.P. 1970. II. 16544, 6 Rev. Tr. Dr. Eur. 376 (1970).

which had held that the French social security authorities were responsible for payment of a widow's pension for death due to a "professional illness" of a French coal miner who had last worked in the Belgian coal mines prior to the discovery that he had silicosis. Instead, said the Social Chamber, article 31(1) of regulation 3 provides that the pension should be paid to his widow by "the competent institution of the state where the risk had been run most recently, which in this case was Belgium."[22]

Professor Lyon-Caen noted that the Social Chamber had slightly changed the language of article 31(1) of regulation 3. The regulation says that "the payments which the victim or his survivors can claim are accorded exclusively under the legislation of the last of the states the conditions of which the interested party has satisfied." He noted that there was no assurance that Gosset had satisfied the requirements of the Belgian law. Professor Lyon-Caen expressed the hope that the Court of Appeal of Rouen to which the case had been remanded would stay its proceedings awaiting a decision of the Belgian authorities as to whether Gosset's widow had the right to benefits under Belgian law. He also noted that in the meantime the French authorities were required to make interim payments to her under article 54(4) of regulation 4 because the conditions of the French legislation had been met.

In *Caisse d'allocations familiales de Maubeuge v. Degousée*,[23] the Social Chamber first held that since French law provides that family assistance payments cannot be made to families whose children reside outside France for a period of more than three months for educational reasons unless the foreign residence was indispensable to the nature of the studies undertaken, such payments are not due to the families of children who spend the week at school in Belgium but return home for weekends and holidays. However, article 40(1) of regulation 3 provides that

A salaried worker or someone assimilated thereto having children who reside or are being raised on the territory of another Member State other than the competent state has the right to receive family allocations for these children according to the provisions of the legislation of the competent state, up to the amount accorded by the legislation of the Member State on the territory of which the children reside or are being raised.

Consequently, the families of children studying in Belgium have a right to family allowances equal to the Belgian payments. The Belgian payments are,

[22] Cass. civ. soc., Feb. 16, 1965, D.S. 1965. Jur. 723 (note Voirin), 55 Rev. Cr. D.I.P. 88 (note Lyon-Caen) (1966).

[23] Cass. civ. soc., June 26, 1969, [1969] Bull. Civ. V. 374. Accord, Caisse d'allocations familiales de Douai v. Venville, Cass. civ. soc., Dec. 11, 1969, [1969] Bull. Civ. V. 579.

to be sure, less than the French, but this is still a more favorable result than that given by the Social Chamber in another case on the same day in which the families of children studying in Geneva for more than three months received no family allowances at all for those children.[24]

In *Antonicelli v. Société de secours minières du Haut-Rhin*,[25] the Social Chamber applied the rule found in article 19 of regulation 3 that hospitalization and other medical charges incurred in another Member State are to be paid by the social security office with which the claimant is affiliated only if the medical care was needed unexpectedly and immediately or if the claimant had previously received an authorization to receive medical care in the other Member State.

In *C.R.A.M. v. Mayer*,[26] the Social Chamber held that when a person claiming old age benefits had worked a sufficient time in France to fulfill the requirements of French law without the need of adding any period of time in another Member State, there is no need to apply articles 27 and 28 of regulation 3, either to determine the eligibility for the benefits or for the purpose of determining the pro-rata share.

In *Dir. rég. sécur. soc. de Lille v. Caisse d'alloc. famil. de Roubaix-Tourcoing*,[27] the Social Chamber had to decide whether a social security office could recover the payments for family allowances made to a person who worked in several of the Member States for a firm whose headquarters were in France and who, although he had declared that he was domiciled in France, resided in Belgium with his family.

It is fortunate for the development of Community law that the courts of the Member States are called on to apply such complex regulations which raise difficult questions of interpretation but no major conflicts with the national law. This is particularly true in France. It has long been expected that the French courts might hesitate to apply Community law with the vigor its advocates would desire. In these social security cases the courts apply Community law with no second thoughts. These cases appear to be of little more significance for them than the host of other cases involving bilateral or multilateral treaties in which "authentic" interpretations are common.

The impact of these cases on the general reception of Community law in the French courts is heightened by the fact that only the court of first instance is a separate court. Appeals go to an ordinary court of appeal and on *cassa-*

[24] Bernard v. Caisse d'allocations familiales d'Arras, [1969] Bull. Civ. V. 374.

[25] Cass. civ. soc., Jan. 14, 1970, D.S. 1970. somm. 118, [1970] Bull. Civ. V. 14. Accord, Dir. rég. séc. soc. de Lille v. Leclercq, Cass. civ. soc., Oct. 6, 1971, D.S. 1972. Jur. 181.

[26] Cass. civ. soc., July 2, 1970, D.S. 1971. somm. 10, Gaz. Pal. 1970. 2. 336.

[27] Cass. civ. soc., Nov. 18, 1971, D.S. 1972. somm. 87.

tion to the regular Cour de Cassation. Although it is true that in most courts of appeal and in the Cour de Cassation the cases are adjudicated by specialized chambers, nevertheless, those chambers are part of the Court of Appeal of Paris, Amiens, etc. and the Cour de Cassation. For this reason the twelve prejudicial questions which have been referred on social security matters, and especially the two from the Cour de Cassation, have permitted the French courts to become familiar with their Community obligation in the least threatening of all possible circumstances.

The Criminal Chamber

The problems raised by Community law are more difficult for the Criminal Chamber and for the Conseil d'État. By the nature of the Criminal Chamber's jurisdiction Community law will necessarily often be raised as a bar to the application of the sanctions enforcing some aspect of French economic law. Similarly in the Conseil d'État the complainant's requested relief has been and in all but the rarest of cases will continue to be the annulment of a provision of French economic law on the basis of its conflict with Community law.[28] Particularly in the first several cases in both tribunals the Community law argument appeared to be a last minute desperate effort to bolster a case feared to be lost on the grounds of French law. Only in the most recent cases have the underlying facts approximated those found in the social security cases, i.e. a collaboration between Community law and French law in which the relevance of the Community regulation was taken for granted and the only question was its meaning in a particular context.

The decisions in the Criminal Chamber and the Conseil d'État have been characterized by five major elements.

1. Neither of the two courts nor the attorneys fully understood the significance of article 177 in the first case to come before them. The casualness with which the obligation to refer a prejudicial question was excluded must simply be written off to inexperience. Later cases have shown more concern, even if they have not shown a propensity to refer questions.

2. In the eyes of both courts the *acte clair* is a perfectly natural and obvious means of screening unnecessary and dilatory requests from litigants for the reference of a prejudicial question.

3. Neither court has been prepared to accept the responsibility for enforcing the formal supremacy of the Constitution, treaties in general, or Community law.

[28] But cf. Comptoir agricole du Pays Bas-Normand, Conseil d'État, Nov. 5, 1971, Rev. Dr. Pub. 718 (1972).

4. The change in the fact patterns in the cases has had more to do with the apparent change in the attitude of the two courts towards Community law than has any other single feature.

5. At all times both courts have indicated their desire to fulfill their obligations under Community law, but they are still unsure what those obligations are. This is particularly true for the Conseil d'État.

The balance of this chapter will be devoted to a description of the cases which have come before the Criminal Chamber and the Conseil d'État. The conclusions to be drawn from these cases will be discussed in the final chapter.

In the *Riff* case, the first Community law case to come before the Criminal Chamber, a bottling company which had occasionally carried the goods of another firm in its trucks was prosecuted for failing to pay certain taxes levied on companies engaging in the private carriage of goods for others. The primary Community law defense raised was that the French tax violated article 80 of the Treaty of Rome which prohibits in respect to transport "any element of support or protection in the interest of one or more particular enterprises or industries...."

In responding to this defense the Criminal Chamber made several questionable statements about the purpose and functioning of specific provisions of substantive Community law.[29] Although it correctly held that article 80 does not prohibit the Member States from levying different rates of taxation on common carriers, contract carriers and private carriers, it incorrectly stated that article 80 serves no purpose other than as a specific application of the prohibition against discrimination based on nationality. Moreover, the Criminal Chamber was also incorrect when it suggested that the penal sanction which punishes a violation of the tax law enacted as a part of the program to coordinate transportation "can be considered" as a "grant in aid" to the coordination of transportation under article 77.[30]

These incorrect assertions of substantive Community law were of little importance in themselves. Of more significance was the Criminal Chamber's assertion "that the court of appeal acted correctly in affirming its jurisdiction to deal with the alleged conflict between the legislation of the Community and municipal law, even though this meant ousting the jurisdiction of the Court of Justice of the European Communities, since article 177 of the Treaty only gives jurisdiction to the Court of Justice over questions concerning the Community's legislation."

This assertion reflected a common understanding in 1964 of the respective

[29] Riff, Cass. crim., Feb. 19, 1964, 92 Clunet 85 (note Jeantet).
[30] For a more complete development of these points see Jeantet, Note, *ibid.*

roles of the Court of Justice and the national courts. *Costa* v. *E.N.E.L.*[31] had not yet been decided and the only relevant decision was *van Gend & Loos* in which the Government of the Netherlands had argued that the Court of Justice was incompetent to answer the question referred to it by the Tariefcommissie on the grounds that it could not decide "whether the provisions of the EEC Treaty should, if necessary, be accorded pre-eminence either over Dutch law or over other agreements ratified by the Netherlands and incorporated in their law." The Court of Justice had responded that "the Court is not called upon to pronounce judgment regarding the application of the Treaty according to the principles of internal Netherlands law, which remains within the jurisdiction of the national courts."[32] The language used by the Criminal Chamber in *Riff* was really not that different.

However, the Criminal Chamber's statement showed that neither it nor the defendant's counsel had understood the extent to which article 177 deviated from the French law of the interpretation of treaties. Since the lower courts have no obligation to refer prejudicial questions under article 177, the Cour de Cassation could not be called upon to decide whether the court of appeal had fulfilled that obligation. The petition for *cassation* should have alleged an incorrect interpretation or application of the substantive Community law. If a problem of interpretation was present, it was up to the Cour de Cassation to refer the prejudicial question itself rather than remand the case to a court of appeal for it to refer the question, as is the practice with the treaties which require Governmental interpretation.

Although *Riff* received little notice when it appeared, the second case to come before the Criminal Chamber was the well known and often commented upon *Brandt* case. It involved a prosecution for the refusal of a merchant to sell to a willing buyer. This prohibition against refusing to sell is in support of the prohibition against price maintenance, an important aspect of the Government's struggle against inflation since the middle 1950s.[33] The case had begun in 1959. It was before the Criminal Chamber for the first time in 1962 when a conviction was quashed on technical grounds.[34]

[31] Costa v. E.N.E.L., Cour de Justice des Communautés Européennes, June 15, 1964, 10 Rec. de la Cour 1141, [1961-1966 Transfer Binder] CCH Comm. Mkt. Rep. ¶ 8023.

[32] N.V. Algemene Transport- en Expeditie Onderneming van Gend & Loos v. The Netherlands Fiscal Administration, Cour de Justice des Communautés Européennes, Feb. 5, 1963, 9 Rec. de la Cour 1, [1961-1966 Transfer Binder] CCH Comm. Mkt. Rep. ¶ 8008.

[33] Art. 37(1)(a) of ordonnance No. 45-1483 of June 30, 1945, added by decree No. 58-545 of June 24, 1958, J.O. 1958. 5877, D. 1958. L. 229. For a general description of the French prohibition against refusal to sell see Bergsten, The Law of Restrictive Trade Practices in France, in 2 Business Regulation in the Common Market Nations (Blake ed. 1969).

[34] Nicolas, Société Brandt et Société Photo Radio Club, Cass. crim., July 11, 1962, D. 1962. Jur. 497 (rapport Costa), S. 1962. Jur. 219 (note Robert).

On January 23, 1963, while the case was on remand to the Court of Appeal of Amiens, the defendant notified the Commission of the EEC of its exclusive dealership concessions with firms in the five other Common Market countries as well as with French concerns. The notification by the defendant was three days prior to the decision of the Court of Appeal of Paris to stay its proceedings in the *Consten-Grundig* case[35] awaiting a determination by the Commission, and eventually by the Court of Justice,[36] on the compatibility of the system of exclusive concessions granted by Grundig to French and other wholesalers.

After the defendant in *Brandt* had notified the Commission of its exclusive concession agreements it requested the Court of Appeal of Amiens to stay the prosecution in order to await a decision of the Commission whether its system of exclusive concessions was legal under article 85 of the Treaty of Rome. Alternatively, it requested the Court of Appeal to refer the question of the legality of the exclusive concessions under article 85.

The Court of Appeal was not sympathetic.[37] It rejected the possibility of a defense based on the Treaty of Rome and any necessity for an interpretation of the Treaty by the Court of Justice, advancing five grounds. First, a refusal by a French seller to sell to a French buyer is not one of those concerted practices likely to affect trade between the Member States. Second, although Brandt, the distributor for France, was prohibited from exporting by its contract with the French manufacturer, there was no prohibition on exports in the exclusive concession contracts between Brandt and the retailers. Therefore, these exclusive concession contracts, which were the contracts Brandt claimed required it not to sell to the complainant, had a purely internal effect. Third, while a contract between two nationals of a Member State may be notified to the Commission, it was not necessary to do so and the defendant could not claim that his optional notification removed the jurisdiction of the national courts to consider the legality of the distribution agreements. In any case the defendant could produce no document indicating that the Commission had commenced proceedings, within the meaning of article 9(3) of Council regulation 17.[38] This was in marked contrast to the *Consten-Grundig* case in which the Commission had made strong overtures to the

[35] Société UNEF v. Ets. Consten, Cour d'appel de Paris, Jan. 26, 1963, D. 1963. Jur. 189 (note Robert), 26 Droit Social 135 (concl. Desangles) (1963).

[36] Ets Consten et Grundig-Verkaufs GmbH v. Commission of the European Economic Community, Cour de Justice des Communautés Européennes, July 13, 1966, 12 Rec. de la Cour 429, [1961-1966 Transfer Binder] CCH Comm. Mkt. Rep. ¶ 8046.

[37] Nicolas et Société Brandt Frères, Cour d'appel d'Amiens, May 9, 1963, D. 1963. Jur. 556 (note Hémard), 52 Rev. Cr. D.I.P. 812 (note Mezger) (1963).

[38] Regulation 17 of Feb. 6, 1962, 5 E.E.C. J.O. 204 (1962).

French government to have the proceedings in the Court of Appeal of Paris suspended until the Commission could consider the legality of the network of concessions in the light of article 85.[39] Fourth, if the Commission were to grant an exemption under article 85(3), that would affect only Community law. It would not in any way affect the prohibition of refusal to sell in French law. Fifth, the Court of Justice is competent only to interpret Community law, but not to rule on any conflict between Community law and national law. On this last point the court of appeal anticipated the language of the Criminal Chamber in *Riff*.

Virtually all of the arguments advanced by the Court of Appeal of Amiens pointed up distinctions between *Consten-Grundig* and *Brandt*. Nevertheless, the court had gone out of its way to exclude the application of Community law even though its application was not beyond the limits of reasonable argument and interpretation of the Treaty.

Except for a minor question of procedure the petition for *cassation* to the Criminal Chamber was based on the alleged conflict between the French prohibition of refusal to sell and article 85 of the Treaty. The Criminal Chamber rejected the petition on the sole basis that the Court of Appeal of Amiens had found as a *fact* that the contracts between the defendant and the French retailers, which offered the basis for the defendant's alleged right to refuse to sell to the complainant, did not affect commerce between the Member States.[40] Since the Cour de Cassation is bound by the findings of fact of the lower courts, there was no legal basis to quash the decision below. Therefore, there was no reason, according to the Criminal Chamber, to consider any of the other reasons given by the court of appeal, even those which were "erroneous." In a note to the case the judge who had been *rapporteur* in the Criminal Chamber emphasized that the action of the court in deliberately not repeating the arguments advanced by Amiens was "taken by the French court, not in a spirit of rebellion towards Community law, but on the contrary in the spirit of collaboration desired by the Advocate General Lagrange."

The decision was, however, troublesome. Even though the Criminal Chamber said that Amiens had found as a fact that the contracts between Brandt, a French company, and the French retailers in regard to goods manufactured in France did not affect commerce between the Member States, that finding was in truth a legal conclusion subject to review. It is not usunual for the Cour de Cassation to disagree with a court of appeal as to whether a

[39] See the conclusions by Desangles, 26 Droit Social 135 (1963).

[40] Nicolas et Société Brandt Frères, Cass. crim., Oct. 22, 1964, D. 1964. Jur. 753 (note Costa), 54 Rev. Cr. D.I.P. 161 (note Mezger) (1965).

finding was one of fact or of law. In this case a true finding of fact would have required an economic analysis of the impact of the system of distribution in France on the trade between the Member States. Anything short of that was an *a priori* conclusion based on policy arguments.[41]

To be fair, however, it is unlikely that the result in the case would have been different if the Court of Justice had been asked a prejudicial question. Even today, much less in 1964, the Communities are not prepared either to legislate directly on distribution agreements wholly within one Member State which do not contain a prohibition on export to other Member States,[42] or to displace the national law of competition absent a fully effective Community law coupled with regulations issued under the authority of article 87.[43] Even though there were potential conflicts between the French law of refusal to sell and article 85, no practical harm was done in the case because of the failure to refer a prejudicial question.

The deficiencies in the opinion of the Criminal Chamber in *Riff* had been due to an unawareness of the significance of Community law. The deficiencies in *Brandt* arose from the impatience of the Court with what appeared to be nothing more than dilatory tactics. *Brandt* was a crucial case in the development of the French law of refusal to sell. It had already been before the French courts for almost five years. If the law prohibiting refusals to sell was to be effective, it was important that this conviction be affirmed. It was un-

[41] Agreements under which an enterprise agrees to obtain its supplies only from one enterprise to the exclusion of all others, do not, merely because of their type, fulfill the conditions for incompatibility with the Common Market contained in Article 85, paragraph 1, of the Treaty. They may, however, fulfill them where, either in isolation or together with others in the economic and legal context in which they were concluded and on the basis of all the objective elements of law or of fact, they are likely to impair trade between Member States and their object or effect is to prevent, restrict, or distort competition.

S. A. Brasserie de Haecht v. Consorts Wilkin-Janssen, Cour de Justice des Communautés Européennes, Dec. 12, 1967, 13 Rec. de la Cour 525, [1967-1970 Transfer Binder] CCH Comm. Mkt. Rep. ¶ 8053. The contract in question required the defendants, the owners of a Belgian cafe, to purchase all of their beer from the plaintiff, a Belgian brewery. Both the Court of Justice and all the parties seemed to accept as a matter of course that it was a question of fact whether an exclusive supply contract between two enterprises in the same Member State did affect trade between the Member States. The problem for the Court of Justice was to determine whether the contract in litigation should be considered in isolation or whether it should be viewed in the light of the general economic situation, including the existence of similar contracts between other breweries and other cafes.

[42] Art. 1(2) of regulation 67/67 of March 22, 1967, 10 E.E.C. J.O. 849/67 (1967).

[43] Walt Wilhelm v. Bundeskartellamt, Cour de Justice des Communautés Européennes, Feb. 13, 1969, 15 Rec. de la Cour 1, [1967-1970 Transfer Binder] CCH Comm. Mkt. Rep. ¶ 8056; Parliamentary resolution of June 7, 1971, 14 E.E.C. J.O. C 66/11 (1971). That the French legislation on retail price maintenance, which includes the prohibition of refusal to sell, does not affect trade between the Member States in the sense of article 85 of the Treaty, see Response to Parliamentary Question No. 247/71, 14 E.E.C. J.O. C 115/5 (1971).

fortunate that it posed the question of the relationship of national law and Community law in such an awkward posture.

Although the Community law defense was also rejected in the next two cases, it was evident that the substance and technique of Community law had penetrated into the French legal system. Both cases involved goods which had originated in third countries but had been imported into France from another Member State. After goods from third countries are once domesticated, they can thereafter circulate freely throughout the other Member States. In *Deroche*, the first of the two cases, the goods had been admitted to the regime of *libre pratique* in Belgium by the payment of the requisite import duties.[44]

The French importer of the goods from Belgium was prosecuted for failure to secure an import license. He claimed that, even though the license was issued automatically and without delay, the requirement of securing a license was a violation of the Community provisions on the free circulation of goods, and in particular articles 9 and 10 on goods coming from third countries and articles 30 and 31 on quantitative restrictions or measures having an equivalent effect. The defendant requested the Criminal Chamber to refer two prejudicial questions. "Does the requirement of an import license for goods under the regime of *libre pratique* constitute a measure *equivalent* to a quantitative restriction? What is the meaning of the expression measures with the equivalent effect to a quantitative restriction in the sense of articles 30 and 31 of the Treaty?"

The Criminal Chamber rejected the request on the grounds that the Court of Justice had already said in *Albatros v. Sopeco* that "none of the articles of the Treaty mentioned [in the questions there posed] implies the abrogation... at the date of the Treaty's entry into force of the quantitative restrictions, discriminations or measures of equivalent effect existing at that date, or obliges the States to carry out their complete abolition as from 1959."[45] The Criminal Chamber justified its reliance on *Albatros* by citing the opinion of the Court of Justice in *Da Costa* that "the authority of an interpretation already given by it in an analogous case can remove the purpose from [the obligation to refer a prejudicial question] and empty it of its content."[46]

[44] Deroche, Cass. crim., June 29, 1966, D.S. 1966. Jur. 595 (rapport Mazard), Gaz. Pal. 1966. 2. 297.

[45] Albatros v. Société des Pétroles et des combustibles liquides, Cour de Justice des Communautés Européennes, Feb. 4, 1965, 11 Rec. de la Cour 3, [1961-1966 Transfer Binder] CCH Comm. Mkt. Rep. ¶ 8029.

[46] Da Costa en Schaake N.V. v. The Netherlands Fiscal Authority, Cour de Justice des Communautés Européennes, March 27, 1963, 9 Rec. de la Cour 59, [1961-1966 Transfer Binder] CCH Comm. Mkt. Rep. ¶ 8010.

Although *Deroche* can be seen as simply the third in the series in which the Criminal Chamber neither recognized a Community law defense nor referred a prejudicial question, it was also the third case in which the Criminal Chamber was correct on the merits.[47] Moreover, we must agree with the *rapporteur* that the Criminal Chamber's extraordinary action of citing by name the two decisions of the Court of Justice "recognize[d] the supranational rank of the Court in Luxemburg."[48]

Six months later in the *Lapeyre* case the Criminal Chamber was again concerned with goods originating in a third country.[49] Unbleached cotton cloth had been imported duty free from Yugoslavia under a procedure for temporary admission during which time further processing could take place prior to re-export.

The cloth was bleached in France and exported to Germany under the Community procedures for "traffic in processed goods." The cloth was then sold to the defendant French firm which imported them as Community goods. The Community rules provide that goods originating in third countries are domesticated if they are transformed by work within a Member State as well as by the payment of import duties. In a verification *a posteriori* the French customs officials determined the import declaration to be fraudulent on two grounds: that the exportation to Germany and reimportation into France was to avoid customs duties fraudulently, and that the amount of work done on them in France had not been sufficient to constitute them French goods, i.e. Community goods. The defendant claimed that bleaching the cloth, which added some 10% to 15% to their value, was an adequate transformation.

For the first time the Criminal Chamber explicitly recognized that its obligation to refer prejudicial questions under article 177 was mandatory whereas that of the court of appeal was discretionary. Nevertheless, the Criminal Chamber did not feel compelled to refer a prejudicial question. An unpublished administrative decision of the Commission had said that "in order to avoid abuses and to assure a uniform application of the provisions of the decision of June 28, 1960, it has been decided to exclude, from the

[47] On December 5, 1966 the Commission presented to the Council a proposed directive by which all licenses, authorizations, visas, attestations, certificates or similar documents would no longer be necessary for goods from third countries which were free to circulate throughout the Communities by virtue of articles 9 and 10 of the Treaty. 10 E.E.C. J.O. 260/67 (1967). On July 8, 1971 the Commission noted that the proposed directive had not yet been adopted and that until it had such documents could be required so long as they were delivered automatically and without delay. Response to Parliamentary Question No. 83/71, 14 E.E.C. J.O. C 68/9 (1971).

[48] Report by Mazard in D.S. 1966 Jur. 595.

[49] Lapeyre v. Administration des Douanes, Cass. crim., Jan. 5, 1967, D.S. 1967. Jur. 465 (rapport Mazard), J.C.P. 1967. II. 15249, 3 Rev. Tr. Dr. Eur. 696 (rapport Mazard) (1967).

benefit of these provisions, as of now, the operations which, because of their unimportance, cannot qualify as 'transformation.'"[50] The decision went on to describe by way of example "washing, painting, etc., which is intended simply to improve the commercial appearance of the imported products or their merchantable quality." The Criminal Chamber held that the clear meaning of the unpublished decision was to exclude minor operation of the type involved in this case from the definition of "transformations."

Finally, in its decision of October 22, 1970, in *Ramel* the Criminal Chamber demonstrated that if the facts were appropriate it did not have any systematic opposition to the application of Community law as a bar to the enforcement of French law.[51] On April 4, 1962, the Council of Ministers took the first step towards the creation of a common market in wine by adopting regulation 24.[52] On the same day it implemented the regulation by a "decision" addressed to Germany, France and Italy in which those three States were required to open contingents for the importation of quality wines from the other Member States.[53] The wine had to come from designated regions, be of a requisite quality and have the necessary certificates from the proper authorities of the exporting Member State. France's obligation under this decision was to import 150,000 hectoliters of wine from Italy.

After the majority of the Italian wine had been resold by the importer, Ramel, it was tested by the French authorities. It was found not to conform to the French law governing unfermented natural wines, as all imported wines must,[54] and Ramel was prosecuted for fraud. The criminal prosecution was joined by civil actions for damages by the Administration for Indirect Taxation and by the trade association for unfermented natural wines. The trial court acquitted Ramel of the criminal charge and dismissed the civil parties, a decision which was affirmed on appeal. The prosecution did not petition the Cour de Cassation to quash the acquittal, but the civil parties petitioned to have quashed the judgment dismissing their civil actions.

Their major argument was that the requirement that wine sold in France as an unfermented natural wine must conform to the French standards for such a designation is part of the tax law and therefore territorial by nature. It was irrelevant whether the wine conformed to the Italian standards.

This argument was rejected by the Criminal Chamber as it had been rejected by the lower courts. The Community regulation and the implementing

[50] Quoted in the report by Mazard, *ibid.*

[51] Administration des contributions indirects v. Ramel, Cass. crim., Oct. 22, 1970, D.S. 1970. Jur. 221 (rapport Mazard, note Rideau), 6 Rev. Tr. Dr. Eur. 750 (1970).

[52] Regulation 24 of April 4, 1962, 5 E.E.C. J.O. 989 (1962).

[53] Decision of April 4, 1962, 5 E.E.C. J.O. 1002 (1962).

[54] Art. 2 of decree No. 63-1001 of Oct. 4, 1963, J.O. 1963. 9015, D. 1963. L. 314.

decision required the importing Member State to accept the certification that the wine conformed to the legislation of the exporting state for the type of wine concerned. The *rapporteur* noted that this was a great inconvenience and led to the inequality of treatment between French and Italian wine when the legislation of the two Member States was significantly different, as it was in this case. Nevertheless, he suggested to the Criminal Chamber that the Community regulation and implementing decision had the status of treaties and that under article 55 of the Constitution treaties "have an authority superior to that of statutes," a position adopted by the Criminal Chamber as its own.

The most striking feature of the decision is that the supremacy of Community law was clearly stated, was specifically said to include both regulations and decisions, involved a Community regulation adopted prior to the French text in question[55] and led to the dismissal of an action based on the violation of an important aspect of French economic law. No result could have been more "Community." The failure to refer a prejudicial question as to the meaning of the Community regulation and decision cannot be faulted on the ground that it was an excuse to preserve the independence of French law. Even the reiteration by the *rapporteur* that it is the national courts and not the Court of Justice which must settle the conflicts between Community law and national law appears as a statement of responsibility to the Community legal system rather than as a rear guard action against an encroaching enemy.

Compared to the Community aspects of the case, the doubts which one might have are minor. Nevertheless, it is disturbing that the *rapporteur* cited the *Riff* case rather than any one of a number of decisions of the Court of Justice for the proposition that the national courts must settle the conflicts between Community law and national law. Similarly, article 55 of the Constitution of 1958, rather than the decision of the Court of Justice in *Costa v. E.N.E.L.*, was cited to uphold the supremacy of Community law. What the French law giveth, the French law can take away.

The Criminal Chamber's most recent decisions demonstrate the extent to which Community law has become the operative norm to which the criminal law must give effect. In *Von Saldern* the Criminal Chamber held that Community regulations had no retroactive effect so as to exonerate actions taken

[55] The Community regulation and decision were dated April 4, 1962 whereas the French decree specifying that imported wine was subject to the French standards was dated October 4, 1963 The French standards themselves were found in earlier texts.

prior to their effective date unless the regulation specifically so states.[56] In *Guerrini* the conviction of an egg merchant for labeling products in a manner violating French law was quashed on the grounds that the adoption of an inconsistent Community regulation had implicitly repealed the French text prior to its subsequent explicit repeal by a French decree.[57] In *Quaak* the conviction of a merchant for failure to label in conformity with the combined provisions of a French decree and a Community regulation was confirmed.[58]

The Conseil d'État

The experience of the Conseil d'État with Community law has been strikingly similar to that of the Criminal Chamber. It began with a case in 1964 after *Riff* and before *Brandt* in which the private party complainant alleged that Community law precluded the application of an aspect of French economic law which long antedated the Communities. The Conseil d'État correctly rejected this argument on the merits but included in its opinion a description of its obligations under Community law which concerned many Community partisans. In the subsequent cases the Conseil d'État has shown an increasing understanding and sympathy for Community law which culminated in the first reference of a prejudicial question in 1970.

The first case was the well-known and often criticized decision in *Shell-Berre.*[59] It involved the law of March 30, 1928, which provides for the regulation of the importation of petroleum and petroleum products into France and, by extension, of the petroleum industry in general. By a decree of January 3, 1959, implemented by an order of the same date, new rules were added regulating the system of distribution.[60]

The companies had to choose one of two methods of determining the extent to which they could open new service stations or introduce their products into existing service stations. Under the "implantation" rule a company could open service stations no closer than 40 kilometers from another station bearing its brand nor closer than 5 kilometers from a group of stations of a different brand. Under the "quota" rule there were no restrictions on the

[56] Von Saldern, Cass. crim., Nov. 10, 1970, D.S. 1971. Jur. 509 (note Mazard), J.C.P. 1971. II. 16714 (note L. S. C.), 7 Rev. Tr. Dr. Eur. 504 (1971).

[57] Guerrini, Cass. crim., Jan. 7, 1972, D.S. 1972. Jur. 497 (note Rideau), J.C.P. 1972. II. 17158 (2e espèce) (note Guérin).

[58] Quaak, Cass. crim., June 13, 1972, D.S. 1972. Jur. 685 (note Rideau).

[59] Société des Pétroles Shell-Berre, Conseil d'État, June 5, 1964, Gaz. Pal. 1964. 2. 35, 20 Act. Jur. Dr. Ad. 438 (note de Laubadère) (1964), 91 Clunet 794 (note de Soto) (1964), 80 Rev. Dr. Pub. 1019 (concl. Questiaux) (1964).

[60] Law of March 30, 1928, J.O. March 31, 1928, D.P. 1929. 4. 137; decree No. 59-95 of Jan. 3, 1959, J.O. Jan. 8, 1959.

location of stations, but each company was limited to the number of stations equal to the total number of tons of petroleum and petroleum products it could import divided by 1000.

Four of the major international oil companies and one independent firm petitioned the Conseil d'État to annul the decree and the order. The essential part of their argument was that the decree and order were an interference with liberty of commerce and equality of treatment. Although these were serious arguments which raised fundamental questions of the compatibility of the dirigist economic policy pursued in an intensive manner in France since the 1930s with an underlying policy of political and economic freedom, the conflict in *Shell-Berre* was resolved in favor of the legitimacy of the new rules under the statute of 1928.[61]

As a final and subsidiary argument by only one of the five petitioners, the decree and order were alleged to violate a number of articles of the Treaty of Rome. The petitioner requested the Conseil d'État to stay its proceedings and refer a prejudicial question of the interpretation of those articles to the Court of Justice. The Government countered with the argument that the system of control over petroleum constituted a state trading monopoly under article 37 of the Treaty, and that any obligations on the part of France to adjust its legislation to the requirements of the Treaty could arise only upon recommendations of the Commission pursuant to article 37(6).

Following the suggestion of its *commissaire du gouvernement* Mme Questiaux, the Conseil d'État applied its standard criterion for the determination whether a prejudicial question was called for. It reiterated that there is no need for one unless there is a "question," by which it meant the existence of a serious doubt over the meaning of a provision necessary to the determination of the case. It then held that it was "clear that the French petroleum legislation was subject to article 37 and was not presently in conflict with the Treaty."

The reaction of the commentators was immediate and universally disapproving.[62] Their argument was not so much that the Conseil d'État had been wrong in its interpretation of article 37, but that there were two viable alternative interpretations from which the Conseil d'État had chosen the one

[61] The broad discretionary authority of the Government over the economy which was recognized in *Shell-Berre* has recently been under concerted attack. See generally, Guibal, *La justification des atteintes à la liberté du commerce et de l'industrie*, 28 Act. Jur. Dr. Ad. 330 (1972); Savy, *Le contrôle juridictionnel de la légalité des décisions économiques de l'administration*, 28 Act. Jur. Dr. Ad. 3 (1972); Delmas-Marsalet, *Le contrôle juridictionnel des interventions économiques de l'état*, 22 Conseil d'État: Etudes et Documents 133 (1969).

[62] See notes cited note 59 *supra*; Chevallier, *Note on the case Soc. des Pétroles Shell-Berre*, 3 Comm. Mkt. L. R. 100 (1965).

which most completely protected the French law from the effects of Community law. Even if the Conseil d'État was ultimately correct on the merits, the matter was not so clear as to absolve it from its obligation to refer a prejudicial question. These sentiments were most forcefully expressed in the title of one of the articles, "The Obscure Clarity of Article 37 of the Treaty of the European Economic Community."[63]

The participants in the debate which followed over the adequacy of the Conseil d'État's formula in a Community context did not start with the same goals. The commentators were anxious that the French courts prove that they would carry out their obligations under Community law in good faith. The best proof of their good faith would be for the courts to refer prejudicial questions whenever there was the slightest argument over the meaning of an applicable Community text. No French court had as yet referred a prejudicial question at the time of *Shell-Berre*, nor was one to do so for another thirteen months. The commentators were becoming anxious.

Those who spoke for the Conseil d'État did not feel it was necessary to demonstrate good faith by referring a prejudicial question when one was not needed to decide the case.[64] The Conseil d'État had decided the *Shell-Berre* case correctly as was demonstrated by the subsequent identical interpretation of article 37 given by the Court of Justice in *Albatros v. Sopeco.*[65] In spite of the Court of Justice's implied rebuke of the Conseil d'État when it commented that it was always appropriate for any litigant to request an interpretation of the "complex" provisions of chapter 2 of the Treaty, of which article 37 is a part, the Conseil d'État did not feel that its function included the reference of prejudicial questions either to enable the Court of Justice to proclaim the meaning of Community law or to reduce the concerns of the commentators that the French courts would not play their role in the development of Community law. Although article 177 provides an opportunity for the national courts and the Court of Justice to cooperate in the disposition of national litigation in such a manner that there will not be a divergence of interpretation, "every case has a deep unity. The dispersion of

[63] Colliard, *L'obscure clarté de l'article 37 du Traité de la Communauté économique européenne*, D. 1964. chron. 263.

[64] Odent, *L'article 177 du Traité de Rome et la jurisprudence du Conseil d'État*, [1965] Bulletin de l'Association des juristes européens, Nos. 23-24, p. 5; 1 Odent, Contentieux administratif, 1965-66, at 236-39; Lagrange, *The European Court of Justice and National Courts: The Theory of the Acte Clair: A Bone of Contention or a Source of Unity?*, 8 Comm. Mkt. L. Rev. 313 (1971). See also the conclusions of Mme Questiaux as *commissaire du gouvernement* in the several cases before the Conseil d'État.

[65] Odent, *L'article 177* at 17.

the questions that it poses is in itself a bad thing. It disfigures the litigation. It must be avoided every time that it is possible to do so."[66]

It was acknowledged that this raises the possibility that there will be some divergence between the Court of Justice and a national court or between two national courts. However, it was pointed out, perfect agreement is not necessary and does not exist even within national legal systems. There are differences in interpretation of French law between the Conseil d'État and the Cour de Cassation, or even between the different chambers of the Cour de Cassation. As was stated by M. Odent, at the time Vice-President of the Section du contentieux,

> One can feel a certain scepticism towards all that is only rules of procedure to eliminate the risks of divergence. It is much more a reciprocal desire for a harmony of conceptions, the mutual respect of competence and of national susceptibilities, and the concern for jurisdictional discipline which will give positive results.[67]

The Conseil d'État was closely watched to see whether it would live up to the standards of "concern for jurisdictional discipline" which Odent had set for it as much as for the Court of Justice. Several of the subsequent cases were routine. In the first the Conseil d'État recognized that article 31, which prohibits "new quantitative restrictions or measures with equivalent effect," is directly applicable.[68] However, it went on to hold that a 1962 notice to milk importers was valid in spite of article 31. The notice established the criteria under which special licenses for the importation of conserved milk from the other Member States were to be granted during a period of a temporary milk shortage in France. The licenses were to be granted only to those importers who agreed not to take a windfall profit from the situation. They had to agree that at a later time they would export milk without an export subsidy to the extent that the amount of the export subsidy they waived would equal the difference between the current French price for milk and the lower price at which they would be able to purchase the conserved milk in the other Member States. There was no suggestion that the obligation to export without subsidy in the future had made it impossible to import the entire quota of conserved milk which had been authorized. If it had, the restriction might have violated the article 31 standstill provision on quantitative restrictions.

[66] *Ibid.* at 15.
[67] *Ibid.* at 17.
[68] Syndicat national des importateurs français des produits laitiers et avicoles, Conseil d'État, Jan. 27, 1967, J.C.P. 1967. II. 15281, 3 Rev. Tr. Dr. Eur. 398 (concl. Bernard) (1967).

In a second case a French decree which established the basis on which taxes were rebated on the exportation of flour was annulled for violation of its authorizing statute.[69] The statute required the decree to be in harmony with a Community regulation. A simple comparison of the decree and the Community regulation demonstrated that they were not in harmony.

In the third case the Conseil d'État held that the obligation of a Member State to inform the Commission and the other Member States of changes in any special tariff regimes existing at the time of the creation of the EEC was not an obligation upon which an individual could rely.[70]

Although all three cases had employed the theory of the *acte clair* to some degree, they had not raised it in a context which caused any substantial concern. However, in two other cases decided by the Conseil d'État the *acte clair* appeared to be used as a device to avoid sending a prejudicial question when one was clearly warranted.

In *Petitjean*,[71] the first of these two cases, the complainants claimed that two parafiscal taxes levied on the production of tomato conserves were illegal.[72] As is often the situation in respect to such cases before the Conseil d'État, no matter how solid the Community law argument, it is subsidiary to other more encompassing arguments based on French law.[73] In *Petitjean* the complainants requested the annulment of the entire tax under French law, but the tax was said to be illegal under Community law only to the extent that it was used to subsidize exports to the other Member States, a subsidy claimed to be illegal either as a prohibited state aid under article 92 or as dumping under article 91.

The *commissaire du gouvernement* Mme Questiaux suggested to the Conseil d'État that the provisions on state aids under article 92 were not self executing. Although article 92 declares such aids incompatible with the Common Market if they distort competition, it goes on to enumerate a number of exceptions. Some of these exceptions require technical economic competence or political judgment which it is not appropriate for a national court to exercise.[74] Moreover, according to article 93 the Commission must

[69] Comité national de la meunerie d'exportation, Conseil d'État, Feb. 15, 1967, J.C.P. 1967. II. 15283, 3 Rev. Tr. Dr. Eur. 404 (concl. Braibant) (1967).

[70] Jammes, Conseil d'État, May 23, 1969, J.C.P. 1969. II. 16020 (obs. Ruzié), 6 Rev. Tr. Dr. Eur. 168 (1970). Cf. Fédération nationale des producteurs de vins de consommation courante, Conseil d'État, March 17, 1971, [1971] Rec. Cons. d'Ét. 215.

[71] Société des établissements Petitjean, Conseil d'État, Feb. 10, 1967, J.C.P. 1967. II. 15282, 3 Rev. Tr. Dr. Eur. 681 (concl. Questiaux) (1967).

[72] Decree No. 62-998 of Aug. 23, 1962, J.O. 1962. 8344.

[73] See Questiaux et Théry, *A propos des taxes parafiscales et de l'organisation des marchés*, 25 Act. Jur. Dr. Ad. 465 (1969).

[74] Cf. Lagrange's conclusions in Costa v. E.N.E.L. in 10 Rec. de la Cour at 1185-86, [1961-Transfer Binder] CCH Comm. Mkt. Rep. ¶ 8023 at 7388.

constantly examine all systems of aid existing in the Member States and call on the Member States to abolish or modify such aid if it is not compatible with the Common Market within the meaning of article 92. Therefore, she concluded that the prohibition of article 92 does not ripen except as a consequence of the action of the Commission authorized by article 93.

It was not as obvious as it appeared from the conclusions of Mme Questiaux that article 92 was not self executing. The prohibition in article 92(1) of aids which distort competition is sufficiently clear and needs no further action by any Community agency to become self executing. So are the exceptions to the prohibition listed in article 92(2). The real difficulty lies in article 92(3) which provides that certain aids "may" be deemed compatible with the Common Market.[75] The determination whether any aids fall within article 92(3) requires judgment which is not appropriate for judicial action. However, it is quite possible to interpret article 92(1) as a self executing prohibition unless the defendant State claims that the aid is one which falls within article 92(3). In that case, and only in that case, the procedure envisioned by article 93 would be necessary before the prohibition became executory.[76]

However that may be, *Petitjean's* notoriety arose from Mme Questiaux's suggestion that the Conseil d'État refer a prejudicial question to determine whether article 91 was or was not self executing since, she said, the answer was not clear from the text of article 91 itself. Article 91 prohibits dumping in another Member State during the transitional period. Dumping can take place only so long as there are artificial trade barriers which make it impossible to reimport the dumped goods into the state of manufacture at the dumped price. Once the transitional period had passed and all tariffs and quantitative restrictions were abolished, the need for dumping legislation on trade between the Member States would have ended. Article 92 prohibiting state aids which distort competition would then presumably suffice.

Like articles 92 and 93, article 91 provides that the Commission shall recommend to the dumping party to end the practice. If the dumping does not stop, the Commission can authorize the injured Member State to take protective measures. Article 91 says nothing about the obligation of the dumping party or its home State prior to the Commission's recommendation.

[75] *Ibid.*

[76] In a related matter the Italian Constitutional Court has held that a statute of the Sicilian Regional Assembly which provided for 2,600,000,000 lira to be used to subsidize losses incurred in the purchase of citrus fruit was unconstitutional in that it violated Italy's obligation under article 93(3) to notify the Commission of any plans to grant aid before those plans were put into effect. Commissario Dello Stato per la Regione Siciliana v. La Regione Siciliana, 9 Comm. Mkt. L. Rep. 35 (Italian Constitutional Court 1969).

From what Odent had previously said it would seem that Mme Questiaux's recommendation would have been sufficient to have guaranteed the reference of a prejudicial question. He had said that the decision was made collegiately. "In this respect, collegiality is an important element because it implies a debate, and this debate will bring out whether there is or not an *acte clair* because if, among the ten persons who compose the Assemblée du contentieux some, be that only a small minority, consider that the stipulation in litigation is not clear, the majority would incline towards obscurity and, consequently, towards the request of an interpretation from the Court of Justice."[77] Apparently Mme Questiaux was not able to convince even a small minority that the provision was obscure, because the Conseil d'État held that neither article 91 nor article 92 was self executing.

While *Petitjean* caused something of a stir because of Mme Questiaux's recommendation to refer a prejudicial question and the Conseil d'État's rejection of the recommendation, there was little comment on the merits of the decision. Perhaps this was because the authorization to use proceeds of the parafiscal tax to subsidize exports was merely an authorization and there was no showing that the proceeds had been so used. Mme Questiaux commented on the difficulty this raised for the Conseil d'État when it is called upon to annul a regulation on the basis of the manner in which the regulation might be implemented.[78] However, in this case there was no executed discrimination against nationals from the other Member States and there might never be.[79]

The storm of protest which *Shell-Berre* had evoked in 1964 again broke forth in 1968 following the decision of the Conseil d'État in *Semoule*.[80] The question was whether the rules applicable to third countries under the Common Agricultural Policy (CAP) were applicable to Algeria or whether France could treat agricultural products from Algeria, in this case semolina, as though they were French. The problem was acute because the Algerian semolina had been imported under a French ordonnance adopted after the CAP came into effect and which was later ratified by statute, thereby giving

[77] Odent, *L'article 177* at 15.

[78] 3 Rev. Tr. Dr. Eur. at 692.

[79] Mme Questiaux's conclusions focussed on the possibility that the proceeds of the parafiscal taxes would be used to subsidize exports to the other Member States. The use of the proceeds to subsidize exports to third countries might also violate Community law. Cf. Commission of the European Communities v. Republic of France, Cour de Justice des Communautés Européennes, Dec. 10, 1969, 15 Rec. de la Cour 523, 2 CCH Comm. Mkt. Rep. ¶ 8105.

[80] Syndicat général de fabricants de semoules de France, Conseil d'État, March 1, 1968, D.S. 1968. Jur. 285 (note Lagrange), J.C.P. 1968. II. 15675, 57 Rev. Cr. D.I.P. 516 (concl. Questiaux) (1968).

the ordonnance the authority of the ratifying statute.[81] The ordonnance was an important part of France's policy to maintain a special relationship with Algeria after it had gained its independence.

On the face of it Algeria was subject to the third country rules of the CAP. The doubt arose because Algeria had been part of France when both the Treaty and the CAP had come into effect. When Algeria became independent two days after the effective date of the CAP, the Member States individually had continued to regard it for some purposes as a Member State pending a commercial agreement. The new agreement is still not in existence at the time of writing in early 1973 and the Communities as a whole have never taken a formal position on Algeria's interim status.[82]

When the Conseil d'État decided that it was clear that the rules applicable to third countries need not be applied to Algeria, there was no question but that it had done so to avoid the possibility which it has dreaded since the Communities became a reality. The interpretation of the Community regulation that Algeria was to be treated as a third country would have brought on a direct conflict between Community law and a later French statute. Moreover, the French provisions were important politically. The fear of the Communities' partisans that the Conseil d'État would deliberately shun all suggestion of the supremacy of Community law seemed to be confirmed.

Finally in the summer of 1970 a case appeared in which the Conseil d'État referred a prejudicial question.[83] The case has a striking similarity to the *Ramel* case in the Criminal Chamber in that the facts in both arose out of the implementation of the CAP. In the case before the Criminal Chamber the Italian wine said to violate French standards had been imported as a first step towards the creation of a common market for wine.[84] The Criminal Chamber had found little difficulty in applying the Community text as a bar to the criminal prosecution even though, as it turned out, the particular French penal provision had been enacted later in time than the Community text. In

[81] Ordonnance No. 62-1088 of Sept. 19, 1962, J.O. 1962. 9181, D. 1962. L. 311, ratified by art. 50 of law No. 63-23 of Jan. 15, 1963, J.O. 1963. 508, D. 1963. L. 49.

[82] It was said that Algeria's decision in early January 1973 to abolish tariff preferences for Community goods "will strengthen the EEC's tendency to consider that all the Member States ought now to apply the 'third country' system to Algeria, abolishing the preferences which France and, to a lesser extent, Germany and the Benelux, continue to grant it without any legal foundation." Agence Europe, Jan. 5, 1973, No. 1194 (new series), p. 4. For a general discussion see Tavernier, *Aspects juridiques des relations économiques entre la C.E.E. et l'Algérie*, 8 Rev. Tr. Dr. Eur. 1 (1972).

[83] Syndicat national du commerce extérieur des céréales, Conseil d'État, July 10, 1970, J.C.P. 1971. II. 16701 (concl. Questiaux, note Ruzié), 6 Rev. Tr. Dr. Eur. 742 (concl. Questiaux) (1970).

[84] Administration des contributions indirects v. Ramel, Cass. crim., Oct. 22, 1970, D.S. 1970. Jur. 221 (rapport Mazard, note Rideau), 6 Rev. Tr. Dr. Eur. 750 (1970).

the case before the Conseil d'État it was necessary to determine whether the French regulations implementing the CAP were in conformity with the Community regulation.

The regulation was one of those adopted every year by the Council of Ministers to establish the support levels and general intervention guidelines in the different agricultural products for that crop year.[85] National regulations are also necessary for the detailed implementation of the Council regulations.

For the 1968-69 crop year the French implementing regulation provided that wheat would be purchased only from those sellers who were registered with the agricultural price support office.[86] To register with the office a seller had to meet certain objective criteria. These criteria had been carefully drafted not to discriminate against sellers from the other Member States. A group of French sellers attacked this provision as it affected soft wheat on the grounds that it was manifestly in conflict with the Community regulation which required the price support office to buy from "all" sellers who had as much as 50 tons of a homogeneous lot. As Mme Questiaux, again the *commissaire du gouvernement*, pointed out, it would appear that the French directive should have been immediately annulled. Nevertheless, there was an argument for saying that "all" did not necessarily mean "all" but meant "some" so long as there was no discrimination between nationals from the other Member States.

After the Court of Justice replied that "all" meant "all", the Conseil d'État annulled the directive.[87]

In the only subsequent case the Conseil d'État held that a claim for damages occurring from the actions of French officials who were enforcing a regulation adopted by the Commission of the European Communities, which regulation allegedly went beyond the authorization given the Commission by the Council of Ministers, was not cognizable by a French administrative tribunal but must be presented to the Communities.[88] This abnegation of the responsibility of the Member State in favor of the responsibility of the Com-

[85] Regulation 1028/68 of July 19, 1968, 11 E.E.C. J.O. L 176/1 (1968), implementing Regulation 120/67 of June 13, 1967, 10 E.E.C. J.O. 2269/67 (1967), which created a common marketing organization for cereales.

[86] Ordonnance No. 67-812 of Sept. 22, 1967, J.O. Sept. 27, 1967, J.C.P. 1967. III. 33437.

[87] Syndicat national du commerce extérieur des céréales v. Office national interprofessionnel des céréales, Cour de Justice des Communautés Européennes, Dec. 17, 1970, 16 Rec. de la Cour 1233, 2 CCH Comm. Mkt. Rep. ¶ 8122. Syndicat national du commerce extérieur des céréales, Conseil d'État, Jan. 27, 1971, D.S. 1971. Jur. 645 (note Rainaud), J.C.P. 1971. II. 16703.

[88] Comptoir agricole du Pays Bas-Normand, Conseil d'État, Nov. 5, 1971, Rev. Dr. Pub. 718 (1972).

munities appears to be authorized as a matter of Community law.[89] Moreover, on the merits of the case it does not appear that the Commission's regulation was unauthorized.[90]

[89] Firma E. Kampffmeyer v. EEC Commission, Cour de Justice des Communautés Européennes, July 14, 1967, 13 Rec. de la Cour 317, [1967-1970 Transfer Binder] CCH Comm. Mkt. Rep. ¶ 8055.

[90] Cf. Einfuhr- und Vorratsstelle fur Getreide und Futtermittel v. Köster, Berodt & Co., Cour de Justice des Communautés Européennes, Dec. 17, 1970, 16 Rec. de la Cour 1161, 2 CCH Comm. Mkt. Rep. ¶ 8127.

CHAPTER V

CONCLUSION

To repeat the opening to Chapter IV, Community law has fared as well in the French courts as one could legitimately have expected. The early concern was exaggerated while the present situation remains ambiguous. The French courts are groping towards the fruitful collaboration with the Court of Justice for which the European Parliament has called.

A fruitful collaboration is not a simple matter. Even in developed federal systems there is a constant tension between the courts and the substantive law of the federal government on the one hand and those of the constituent states or provinces on the other. This tension is bound to be particularly evident during the early years of a new political-legal structure such as the European Communities where the locus and scope of decision making and enforcement are still in the formative stages.

The reason usually given for the obligation of the national courts to vindicate the rights of individuals under Community law even in the presence of an inconsistent subsequent national statute is that Community law must be applied uniformly throughout the Member States. This is indeed an important reason, but it is not the ultimate reason. For a long time in the future the differences between the economic and commercial law of the Member States will continue to be so great that any differences in the interpretation of the Community law or the consequences arising out of inadvertent conflicts between Community law and subsequent national statutes will pale in comparison.

The ultimate reason that the courts of the Member States must vindicate the rights of individuals under Community law and thereby recognize the effective superiority of Community law over their national law is that an atmosphere of mutual trust must be established if the Communities are to succeed. The degree of mutual trust necessary to forge a Community is difficult to achieve between sovereign states. It must be carefully nurtured. In particular it can easily be damaged by any indication that the Member

States will not fulfill the bargains already made which have found their way into Community law.

It was recognized from the beginning that the deliberate or inadvertent enactment of national legislation in conflict with Community law would cause a loss of confidence. The surprise was the significance attached to the work of the national courts. Courts which were used to working in relative isolation found themselves under attack, not only from the national specialists in their area of law, but from foreign commentators and politicians as well. The strong reaction to the decision of the Italian Constitutional Court in *Costa* v. *E.N.E.L.*[1] and to the decision of the French Conseil d'État in *Shell-Berre* and *Semoule*[2] was not caused by a conviction that the national legislation in those cases was in violation of Community law. The strong reaction was caused by the indication that the courts would enforce the national legislation whether or not it was in violation of Community law. As a result of the attitude of these courts neither Italy nor France appeared to be as trustworthy a partner. Odent's defense of the Conseil d'État's action in *Shell-Berre* on the grounds that the Court of Justice later interpreted article 37 of the Treaty of Rome in the same manner as had the Conseil d'État was to that extent not responsive to the concern which had been expressed.[3]

On the other hand Odent's defense was not irrelevant to an understanding of the attitude of the French courts towards Community law. They have not been hostile. While prejudicial questions might have been asked in several cases in which they were not, the failure to do so was truly bothersome in only one case, *Semoule*. Even that case need not be repeated if the proper measures are taken.

Certainly the French courts which consider social security matters cannot be faulted for the manner in which they have reacted to the Community regulations. They have referred twelve prejudicial questions and have consistently applied Community law as the governing law whenever it seemed appropriate. This cannot be laid to any particular appreciation of Community law on their part which goes beyond that of the other French courts. It is simply that social security treaties are to social security law in France what tax treaties are to tax law in the United States. The domestic statutes anticipate that treaties have been or will be concluded to modify the statute

[1] Rac. Uff. Corte Cost. 82 (1964), 87 Foro Ital. I, 465 (1964), English translation in [1964] Comm. Mkt. L. R. 425.

[2] Société des Pétroles Shell-Berre, Conseil d'État, June 5, 1964, 20 Act. Jur. Dr. Ad. 438 (note de Laubadère) (1964), 91 Clunet 794 (note de Soto) (1964), 80 Rev. Dr. Pub. 1019 (concl. Questiaux) (1964); Syndicat général de fabricants de semoules de France, Conseil d'État, March 1, 1968, D.S. 1968. Jur. 285 (note M. L[agrange]), J.C.P. 1968. II. 15675, 57 Rev. Cr. D.I.P. 516 (concl. Questiaux) (1968).

[3] Odent, *L'article 177* at 17.

in respect to certain foreign transactions. While questions of supremacy are always imminent, the day to day problem is simply one of legislative intent.

Since the social security treaties often call for active cooperation between the authorities of the contracting states, the representatives of the Governments tend to be in regular contact with one another. They are constantly interpreting the treaties for the purpose of coordinating their activities. The administrative commission created by article 43 of regulation 3 which is charged with the interpretation of the regulation is only a highly formalized example.[4] As a result the French courts have long been in the habit of referring to the Government prejudicial questions of the rights of foreigners under social security treaties. In this light the error of the Court of Appeal of Douai in attempting to refer a prejudicial question to the administrative committee created by article 43 of regulation 3 takes on a new meaning.[5] The court found it completely logical that the interpretation of a multinational regulation should be interpreted by a multinational committee of high level administrators. It has been no more difficult for other French courts to request an interpretation of the social security regulations from a multinational court like the Court of Justice.

It is more difficult for a criminal court to assimilate a treaty. The function of the criminal courts is to enforce the policy of the state as it is expressed in its criminal statutes, while at the same time guaranteeing to the accused adequate procedural safeguards. The treaty does not normally come in aid of the French policy expressed by the criminal statute, as a social security treaty comes in aid of the French social security policy. Instead, in all but the rarest of cases the treaty has been argued as a bar to the prosecution.

The criminal courts could have taken any one of three attitudes towards such treaties. As defenses to a criminal action they could have been construed broadly. Alternatively, the courts could have construed the treaties narrowly so as to preserve the broadest possible application of the general French policy expressed by the criminal statute since a defense based on a treaty is a defense which operates selectively only in favor of those foreigners who can rely upon the same or a similar treaty. The result in fact has been one of abdication. The criminal courts apply the French criminal statute unless and only to the extent that the Government, speaking through the

[4] Regulation 3 of Sept. 25, 1958, 1 E.E.C. J.O. 561 (1958), replaced by art. 80 of regulation 1408/71 of June 14, 1971, 14 E.E.C. J.O. L 149 (1971).

[5] Caisse rég. assurance vieillesse du Nord v. Torrekens, Cour d'appel de Douai, Oct. 8, 1963, D. 1964. Jur. 299 (note R. M. Ch.).

Minister of Foreign Affairs, indicates that its application is precluded by the terms of a treaty.[6]

Although Community law is similar to this model in that it has also been raised as a bar to the prosecution of French criminal law, it differs profoundly in that it does not act as a selective bar. Instead, it supercedes French policy as expressed in the French criminal law and does so in respect to all persons including French citizens. Community law becomes the expression of a higher French policy. Therefore, there is little reason for the criminal courts to resist its application.

This is evident in four recent cases in the Criminal Chamber, all of which involved the allegation of fraud in the importation of goods from other Member States. In all four cases the French law had been violated. In *Deroche* no Community regulation yet existed to prohibit the French requirement that importers secure a license to import goods which were under the regime of *libre pratique* and the conviction was sustained.[7] In *Lapeyre* a Community rule existed which potentially barred the French prosecution for labeling as Community goods cloth which had originally come from Yugoslavia, but a Commission interpretation rendered the Community rule inapplicable.[8] In *Ramel* the regulation under which the Italian wine was imported required the French authorities to accept the Italian standards for the quality of the wine, as was done.[9] Finally, in *Guerrini* a conviction was quashed on the grounds that the French provision had been abrogated by a Community regulation.[10]

These four cases represent one aspect of the future, but the relationship between Community law and French criminal law goes even further. Some Community law requires a criminal sanction to make it effective, but the Communities have no criminal authority of their own. The obvious solution is for the Member States to provide that the violation of particular Community norms constitute violations of the domestic criminal law. This technique, which has been adopted by France, appears in the most recent decision, *Quaak*, in which the substantive rule for which the defendant was convicted

[6] Cf. Piot, Intervention in the Travaux du comité français de Droit International Privé 1958-59 at 119-20.

[7] Deroche, Cass. crim., June 29, 1966, D.S. 1966. Jur. 595 (rapport Mazard), Gaz. Pal. 1966. 2. 297.

[8] Lapeyre v. Administration des douanes, Cass. crim., Jan. 5, 1967, D.S. 1967. Jur. 465 (rapport Mazard), J.C.P. 1967. II. 15249, 3 Rev. Tr. Dr. Eur. 696 (rapport Mazard) (1967).

[9] Administration des contributions indirects v. Ramel, Cass. crim., Oct. 22, 1970, D.S. 1970. Jur. 221 (rapport Mazard, note Rideau), 6 Rev. Tr. Dr. Eur. 750 (1970).

[10] Guerrini, Cass. crim., Jan. 7, 1972, D.S. 1972. Jur. 497 (note Rideau), J.C.P. 1972. II. 17158 (2e espèce) (note Guérin).

was to be found in a Community regulation.[11] It is obvious that the relationship between Community law and French criminal law is approaching that already evident in respect to social security.

The problems are much greater for the Conseil d'État. The relief requested is not the allocation of a relatively small amount of money, as in the social security cases, or the acquittal of an individual or firm, as in the criminal cases. The usual relief requested is the annulment of a provision of French law.

This in itself does not preclude the application of Community law. As Odent pointed out in 1965, the Conseil d'État will annul administrative acts, including regulations of various types, if they conflict with a treaty.[12] It does not matter whether the regulation is prior or subsequent to the treaty. If there was any doubt whether this general rule would be applied to Community law, it has since been dispelled.[13]

But this does not solve all the problems. The Conseil d'État is vitally concerned over the implications of Community law for the supremacy of Parliament. The Conseil d'État has built its authority over the executive by holding it strictly to the requirements enacted by Parliament. When it finally recognized treaties as positive law having the authority of a statute, it was in large part because treaties must receive the approval of Parliament before they can be ratified. But this leads only to the equality of treaty and statute, not to the supremacy of the treaty over the statute.

In the context of the Communities the problem becomes even more acute in one important respect. The French Parliament would not only lose its authority over matters covered by the Community Treaties, but future decisions would be in the hands of the Governments of the Member States with no role – at least for the present time – for any elected parliament in the Community law making process. Although Council regulations, directives and decisions are said to partake of the Treaty they implement, and therefore of the parliamentary ratification of the Treaty, they remain the immediate expression of the Governments of the Member States. It is unlikely that the Conseil d'État would recognize the formal supremacy of this new form of executive action over inconsistent legislation by the French Parliament if the

[11] Quaak, Cass. crim., June 13, 1972, D.S. 1972. Jur. 685 (note Rideau). The problem is discussed in more detail in Johannes, *Le Droit pénal et son harmonisation dans les Communautés Européennes*, 7 Rev. Tr. Dr. Eur. 315 (1971); Bigay, *L'application des règlements communautaires en droit pénal français*, 7 Rev. Tr. Dr. Eur. 53 (1971); Rideau, Note to Guerrini, Cass. crim., Jan. 7, 1972, D.S. 1972. Jur. 497.

[12] Odent, *L'article 177* at 18.

[13] Syndicat national du commerce extérieur des céréales, Conseil d'État, Jan. 27, 1971, D.S. 1971. Jur. 645 (note Rainaud), J.C.P. 1971. II. 16703.

French statute was later in time. The attitude which the Conseil d'État would have if a directly elected European Parliament were significantly involved in the creation of Community law is something which is probably unknown even to the members of the Conseil d'État.

The problems go beyond the implications for parliamentary democracy in the Community context alone. The Conseil d'État, as exemplified most clearly by the conclusions of Mme Questiaux in *Semoule*, finds it difficult to distinguish the claim for Community supremacy from the general claim of treaty supremacy under article 55 of the Constitution. Therefore, the recognition of the supremacy of Community law would, in the present view of the Conseil d'État, bring as a natural consequence the supremacy of all treaties over statutory law. However, Mme Questiaux suggested,

> It is difficult to imagine that there should be created in all the areas affected by an international treaty whole zones in which the laws would be deprived of effect by the judge, and on the basis of texts which he is not fully entitled to interpret. The argument is enticing in order to encourage the development of a Community legal order; its evolution is more difficult to imagine if it withdraws from the action of the legislator whole sections of the life of the country because treaties have appeared in the area in question, the interpretation of which belongs to the Minister of Foreign Affairs.[14]

The authority of the Minister of Foreign Affairs to interpret treaties in one important respect gives the Government more unbridled authority than it received through the extension of Governmental law making powers in the Constitution of 1958. The ordonnances adopted by the Government under the authority of the Constitution are at least subject to judicial review by the Conseil d'État. However, the interpretation of a treaty by the Minister of Foreign Affairs is one executive act specifically beyond the authority of the Conseil d'État to review at the present time.

Even if there was a directly elected European Parliament with significant law making powers there is some question whether the Conseil d'État would feel that it was the appropriate court to determine that a French statute enacted subsequent to the adoption of a Community norm could not be enforced. Every French court is a court of limited jurisdiction. In the case of the Conseil d'État it has jurisdiction over administrative acts. Other courts have jurisdiction over other aspects of French law.

According to one theory the reason why there is no judicial review of the constitutionality of statutes is because there is a court missing in the French

[14] 57 Rev. Cr. D.I.P. 516, 525 (1968), [1970] Comm. Mkt. L. R. 395, 405.

hierarchy.[15] There is no constitutional court, though the Constitutional Council first created in 1946 and strengthened in 1958 is the beginning of such a tribunal. But the very existence of the Constitutional Council indicates that the existing tribunals, including the Conseil d'État, are not expected to rule on the constitutionality of statutes.

There is no missing court in the Community structure. The Court of Justice can adjudicate whether national legislation is in conformity with Community law and the Member States are required to conform to that judgment. As Odent points out, "even if the national courts are mistaken [in their judgment that a national law was not in conflict with Community law], the Court of Justice will always have the last word if the Commission or a Member State seizes it. Community law will thus always win out."[16]

Similarly in her conclusions in *Semoule* Mme Questiaux explained to the Conseil d'État that

> recourse to the coercive procedure laid down in article 169 et seq. of the Treaty when a State misconstrues its obligations is, in a case like this one, the best means for knowing whether the Member States, which have not provided means for leaving the Community, object to the transitional measures of the French State.[17]

The refusal to review the compatibility of a subsequent French statute with Community law is not, then, because of a systematic hostility to Community law, but because "the administrative court cannot make the effort which is asked of it without altering, by its mere will, its institutional position."[18] From the viewpoint of the Conseil d'État, it is the Court of Justice which must make the determination whether a subsequent national statute violates Community law; the Conseil d'État does not have the institutional authority to do so.

As a result of these considerations a constitutional amendment has recently been proposed in the Conseil d'État which would permit the courts to refer a prejudicial question on the conflict between a treaty and a statute to the Constitutional Council.[19] Such a development would provide a means by which the supremacy of treaties, and thereby Community law, could be assured with no major adjustments in the institutional role of the existing tribunals. There is good reason to doubt, however, whether any such constitutional amendment will be adopted in the near future.

[15] Favoreu, Du déni de justice en droit public français 217-269 (1964).
[16] Odent, *L'article 177* at 17.
[17] 57 Rev. Cr. D.I.P. 516, 525 (1968), [1970] Comm. Mkt. L. R. 395, 405.
[18] *Ibid.* at 524, [1970] Comm. Mkt. L. R. 395, 404.
[19] Dubouis, *Le juge administratif français et les règles du droit international*, [1971] Ann. Fr. Dr. Int'l 9, 53; Odent, Contentieux administratif, 1970-71 at 131.

The discussion of parliamentary supremacy has taken on a symbolic importance for the participants far beyond its intrinsic importance. The issue of parliamentary supremacy will seldom come before the Conseil d'État, and steps can be taken to reduce even further the number of those occasions. The deliberate enactment of statutes in conflict with Community law will be rare, and need not trouble us. Such acts will cause a Community constitutional crisis of a greater or lesser extent and the techniques for resolving the crisis will depend on the factors present at the time.

Careful review by the Conseil d'État, among others, should eliminate all but the most obscure conflicts from Government sponsored bills prior to their submission to Parliament. Moreover, the subjects on which Parliament can legislate are not such that many conflicts with Community law are likely. Most legislation susceptible of conflict is enacted by the Government, either under its own constitutionally granted authority or by virtue of a delegation of authority by the Parliament under article 38 of the Constitution to adopt ordonnances in implementation of France's obligations to the Communities.[20] All such executive legislation can be annulled by the Conseil d'État if it is in conflict with Community law unless and until it is ratified by a statute. Moreover, the ratifying statute could be worded in such a way that it would ratify ordonnances only to the extent that they were in conformity with France's obligations under Community law. If this were done, the Conseil d'État could subsequently determine whether an ordonnance, even though apparently ratified, was in conformity with Community law.

Nevertheless, this is a restricted role for the Conseil d'État, a role which is more restricted than is to its liking. Although the rule that the national courts of last resort must refer prejudicial questions will aid in unifying the interpretation of Community law, one cost is a certain ambivalence of the Conseil d'État towards both the Court of Justice and Community law. The Conseil d'État created French administrative law. Now it foresees the possibility that it may become little more than a registrar for the decisions of the Court of Justice just as it has been in large measure for those of the Minister of Foreign Affairs. However, treaties affect French administrative law in only an incidental way whereas Community law promises to displace large segments of it and to become the underlying text for other portions. It is no surprise, therefore, that even though the Conseil d'État is precluded from participating in the development of Community law through the interpretation of Community acts, it still intends at least to decide whether the Com-

[20] For the Government's constitutionally granted authority to legislate see art. 37. The most recent delegation of authority to legislate by ordonnance is contained in Law No. 69-1169 of Dec. 26, 1969, J.O. 1969. 12670, J.C.P. 1970. III, 36218.

munity law is clear or whether it needs interpretation. "It is up to [the judge] to decide, in accordance with his moral responsibility, in all independence and in good conscience, on the clarity or the ambiguity of a provision."[21]

The dispute over the *acte clair* has concentrated on a false problem. By now it is well understood that the national courts of last resort must exercise some judgment whether a prejudicial question is necessary. The debate is now only over the extent of doubt permissible before a Community text is no longer clear and the extent to which the national courts are apt to use the *acte clair* to avoid referring prejudicial questions.

At the present time only the national courts can decide the extent of doubt permissible before a Community text is no longer clear. Similarly, there are no institutional controls to prevent them from using the doctrine of the *acte clair* as a device to avoid referring prejudicial questions. At one time these seemed to be fundamental weaknesses which could be remedied only by radical institutional changes, changes which are unlikely to occur in the near future. However, now that courts of last resort from all six Member States have referred prejudicial questions the problem no longer seems as acute as it once did.

Nevertheless, there are two simple measures which could be taken which would increase Community control over the use of article 177 by the national courts of last resort. The first would be for the Court of Justice to create a Community law doctrine equivalent to the *acte clair*. The doctrine could be called the *texte clair*. Since it would be a Community doctrine, the Court of Justice could spell out the circumstances under which a national court could invoke the *texte clair* so as to be relieved of the obligation to refer a prejudicial question. Although the elaboration of such a doctrine would constitute little more than the substitution of one name for another, it would emphasize that the determination whether a provision of Community law is clear or requires interpretation is a matter which must be decided with Community criteria in mind. It would also reject the claim which has been made that the procedure for the reference of prejudicial questions under article 177 was taken from French administrative law complete with the *acte clair* as it has been known to the Conseil d'État.[22]

The second and more significant change would allow some appropriate Community official, probably from the Commission, to communicate with the national courts of last resort through the Government of the Member

[21] Odent, *L'article 177* at 15.

[22] Odent, *L'article 177* at 15. In a comment on Odent's speech Catalano, a former judge on the Court of Justice, claimed that "article 177 ... was inspired by the Italian procedure for prejudicial questions of a constitutional order...." Catalano, *Intervention, ibid.* at 42.

States whenever it was believed that a Community law question before the court was not clear.[23] In such case the national court could be required to refer the prejudicial question. This would be no more of a interference with the legal proceeding in the national courts than was caused by the Community when they strongly urged the French Government to request the Court of Appeal of Paris stay its proceedings in the *Consten-Grundig* case in order to await a decision by the Commission on the compatibility of the Grundig concession agreements with article 85 of the Treaty of Rome.[24]

Although such measures or similar possibilities might be of some value, they might also do more harm than good. "The climate in which the Community will develop will obviously depend completely on whether Community law is the result of cooperation between the Court of Justice and the national courts or will be imposed by the Court of Justice on more or less reticent national courts."[25]

The climate just as obviously is not wholly dependent on the Court of Justice, but also on the actions of the national courts. So far the civil and criminal courts in France have found it possible to cooperate with the Court of Justice. It is not clear yet the extent to which the Conseil d'État will be able to solve the problems which have kept it from being as cooperative.

They are obviously trying. The proposal to amend the Constitution so that a court could refer a prejudicial question on the conflict between a statute and a treaty to the Constitutional Council, a procedure which would allow for the consecration of the formal supremacy of treaties over statutes pursuant to article 55 of the Constitution, is a major effort in that direction. Furthermore, the decision to send a prejudicial question to the Court of Justice in a case in which the problem of interpretation was much less difficult than it was in *Shell-Berre* or in *Semoule* where no question was asked was more than a simple gesture in a case of minimal importance. It was a pledge of active cooperation in the development and application of Community law.

[23] This suggestion has been previously made in Mok, *The Interpretation by the European Court of Justice of Special Conventions Concluded Between the Member States*, 8 Comm. Mkt. L. Rev. 485, 490 (1971).

[24] Société UNEF v. Ets. Consten, Cour d'appel de Paris, Jan. 26, 1963, D. 1963. Jur. 189 (note Robert), 26 Droit Social 135 (concl. Desangles) (1963).

[25] Odent, *L'article 177* at 20.

APPENDIX

FRENCH CASES POSING PREJUDICIAL QUESTIONS

Syndicat national du commerce extérieur des céréales, Conseil d'État, July 10, 1970, D.S. 1971. Jur. 576 (note Fromont), J.C.P. 1971. II. 16701 (note Ruzié), 6 Rev. Tr. Dr. Eur. 742 (concl. Questiaux) (1970).

Caisse rég. séc. soc. du Nord-Est v. Goffart, Cass. civ. 2e, April 27, 1967, D.S. 1967. Jur. 541 (concl. Schmelck), 74 Rev. Gén. Dr. Int'l Pub. 242 (1968).

Caisse rég. séc. soc. du Nord v. Torrekens, Cass. civ. soc., Oct. 24, 1968, 5 Rev. Tr. Dr. Eur. 138 (1969), 32 Droit Social 331 (obs. Lyon-Caen) (1969).

La Hessische Knappschaft v. Maison Singer, Cour d'appel de Colmar, June 1, 1965, J.C.P. 1966. II. 14578 (2e espèce), Gaz. Pal. 1965. 2. 102.

La Technique Minière, L.T.M. v. Société Maschinenbau Ulm, Cour d'appel de Paris, July 7, 1965, J.C.P. 1966. II. 14578 (4e espèce), Gaz. Pal. 1965. 2. 90 (concl. Toubas).

Ciechelski v. Caisse rég. séc. soc. du Loiret, Cour d'appel d'Orléans, Dec. 22, 1966, Gaz. Pal. 1967. 1. 12, 3 Rev. Tr. Dr. Eur. 407 (1967).

Colditz v. Caisse d'assurance vieillesse des travailleurs salariés, Cour d'appel de Paris, Jan. 28, 1967, unpublished, decision of Dec. 8, 1967 after interpretation by the Cour de Justice, Gaz. Pal. 1969. 1. 50.

Caisse d'assurance vieillesse des travailleurs salariés de Paris v. Duffy, Cour d'appel de Paris, June 27, 1969, Gaz. Pal. 1970. 1. 305.

Murru v. Caisse nationale d'assurance maladie de Paris, Cour d'appel de Paris, unpublished, decision of the Cour de Justice of June 6, 1972, 18 Rec. de la Cour —.

Société Cadillon v. Société Hoss, Tribunal de commerce de Lyon, Sept. 24, 1970, 7 Rev. Tr. Dr. Eur. 212 (1971).

Société Beguelin Import Co. v. G. K. Import-Export, Tribunal de commerce de Nice, unpublished, decision of the Cour de Justice of Nov. 25, 1971, 17 Rec. de la Cour 949, 2 CCH Comm. Mkt. Rep. ¶ 8149.

Société Manpower v. Caisse prim. d'ass. maladie de Strasbourg, Commission de première instance du contentieux de la sécurité sociale et de la mutualité sociale agricole du Bas-Rhin, June 17, 1970, decision of April 21, 1971 after interpretation by the Cour de Justice, J.C.P. 1972. II. 17025.

Gross v. Caisse régionale d'assurance vieillesse des travailleurs salariés de Strasbourg, Commission de première instance du contentieux de la sécurité sociale et de la mutualité sociale agricole du Bas-Rhin, unpublished, decision of the Cour de Justice of Nov. 10, 1971, 17 Rec. de la Cour 871.

Keller v. Caisse régionale d'assurance vieillesse des travailleurs salariés de Strasbourg, Commission de première instance du contentieux de la sécurité sociale et de la mutualité sociale agricole du Bas-Rhin, unpublished, decision of the Cour de Justice of Nov. 10, 1971, 17 Rec de la Cour 885.

Höhn v. Caisse régionale d'assurance vieillesse des travailleurs salariés de Strasbourg, Commission de première instance du contentieux de la sécurité sociale et de la mutualité sociale agricole du Bas-Rhin, unpublished, decision of the Cour de Justice of Nov. 10, 1971, 17 Rec. de la Cour 893.

Merluzzi v. Caisse primaire centrale d'assurance maladie de la région parisienne, Commission de première instance du contentieux de la sécurité sociale et de la mutualité sociale agricole de Paris, unpublished, decision of the Cour de Justice of March 22, 1972, 18 Rec. de la Cour 175.

INDEX

GPSR Compliance

The European Union's (EU) General Product Safety Regulation (GPSR) is a set of rules that requires consumer products to be safe and our obligations to ensure this.

If you have any concerns about our products, you can contact us on ProductSafety@springernature.com

In case Publisher is established outside the EU, the EU authorized representative is:

Springer Nature Customer Service Center GmbH
Europaplatz 3
69115 Heidelberg, Germany

Batch number: 10830943

Printed by Printforce, the Netherlands